MW00623153

MEN

OF

COVENANT

OTHER BOOKS IN THIS SERIES

Men of Valor
Men of Influence

MEN

OF

COVENANT

Oaths, Covenants, and
Transcendent Promises

ROBERT L.
MILLET

DESERET
BOOK

SALT LAKE CITY, UTAH

Library of Congress Cataloging-in-Publication Data

Millet, Robert L., author.
    Men of covenant : oaths, covenants, and transcendent promises / Robert L. Millet.
        pages cm
    Includes bibliographical references and index.
    ISBN 978-1-62972-030-2 (hardbound : alk. paper)
1. Mormon men—Religious life. 2. Priesthood—Mormon Church. 3. The Church of Jesus Christ of Latter-day Saints—Doctrines. 4. Mormon Church—Doctrines. I. Title.
    BX8659.M543 2015
    289.3'320811—dc23   2014048827

Printed in the United States of America
RR Donnelley, Crawfordsville, IN

10   9   8   7   6   5   4   3   2   1

Brethren, pow'r by earthly standards
Comes by rank or wealth or sword;
But the pow'r above all others
Is the priesthood of our Lord.

It is ours, the total armor—
Priesthood held by Christ, our Lord—
If, as brethren, we are worthy
Of the Spirit's whispered word.

Let us venture forth in freedom
With the priesthood as our guide—
Deacons, teachers, priests, and elders,
Seeking virtue side by side.
(*Hymns,* no. 320)

CONTENTS

Contents

ACKNOWLEDGMENTS

AFTER SOME EXPERIENCE IN WRITING, one begins to appreciate just how futile and frustrating it is to acknowledge specifically all the individuals who have been helpful in the preparation of a book. It isn't just that someone important may be overlooked, which is painful enough, but it's also that it is so seldom—indeed, it's quite rare—that a writer has a completely original idea. Of course it is incumbent on an author to give proper attribution for specific sources quoted from or otherwise drawn upon, and yet so very many ideas, concepts, doctrines, precepts, and scriptural applications are in the larger public realm. Is that surprising, given that we live in the prophesied day when the Spirit of the Lord is poured out upon all flesh? (see Joel 2:28–30).

But let me now, having given voice to my concern, express thanks to great priesthood leaders for more than half a century whose articulation of the principles and doctrine of the priesthood has been indelibly stamped on my soul; to my dear friends Lisa Roper and Suzanne Brady at Deseret

Book Company for their encouragement and skillful nurture of this project from concept to completion; to Shauna, my beloved and patient eternal priesthood companion, for creating a spiritual and emotional climate in our home that not only permits but fosters serious and sacred thought; and, most important, to the Lord Jesus Christ, the "Apostle and High Priest of our profession" (Hebrews 3:1), whose priesthood we hold and on whose errand we labor.

Introduction

WE ARE A COVENANT PEOPLE

ONE FRIDAY EVENING MY WIFE, Shauna, and I decided, after a long and hectic week, that we wanted to just sit and watch a couple of old movies to clear our heads and rest our weary bodies. As we watched, we noticed that often one of the main characters attempted to strengthen his or her point by adding, "I promise." In one case, a father took his four-year-old into his arms to comfort her; it was a war scene, and the enemy was drawing nearer as the moments passed. As the dad sought to dry the little girl's tears, he said, "Don't cry, honey. We're all going to be just fine. Nothing is going to happen to us. I promise." Later in that same movie, the father, the main character, was required to leave his family and travel across a precarious and dangerous war zone to get help, a distance of some ten miles. He embraced his adoring but fearful wife and reassured her, "Now don't you worry about a thing. I'll be just fine. I promise."

The second movie was a story of how a devoted coach took a rather unpolished football team and led them, gradually and painfully, to the state championship game. As the two teams headed into their locker rooms at halftime, his team was down by twenty points. The coach expressed his love to the boys, told them just how proud of them he was, commended them for the remarkable progress they had made in the last ten weeks, and then said, "Now I know that things look rather bleak right now, but I have complete confidence in you. I know that our hard work and our intensive training are going to pay off. Now, let's get back on that field. We are going to win this one. I promise."

"I promise." A simple expression, to be sure. And it's an encouraging word, a reassurance. But in both cases the one providing the reassurance, though he clearly meant well, did not have control over all the variables in that environment. Their words were thus more of a hope, a wish, a motivational thought than a statement of fact. Unless the dedicated father or the inspiring coach knew by revelation, had seen in vision the promised outcome, what he promised was not necessarily within his power to deliver. Such a promise was thus quite risky. In that sense, and under these kinds of circumstances, promises can be cheap.

It is not uncommon in our day to listen to a religious program on the radio or watch on television a charismatic preacher deliver an inspirational message and then, at the close of his sermon, call upon listeners to "make a commitment for Christ" or "make a decision for Jesus." These are worthwhile endeavors, noble invitations, for truly each one of us needs to decide how we are going to live our lives, to what cause we will devote ourselves, to what Person or persons we will yield our heart and will. Commitments and decisions are pretty important, aren't they?

But other kinds of promises go much deeper than a casual "I promise" or an "I commit." These promises are covenants, two-way sacred arrangements and assurances between Deity and his people. Covenants are initiated by God. The particulars of the covenant are specified by God. The Almighty sets the terms and conditions. And while a covenant is a spiritual arrangement intended to establish expectations and foster resolve and dedication on the part of mortals, it is far more than a transaction between the two parties. A covenant, in the gospel sense, is one of the means by which our infinite and eternal Father in Heaven links himself with his children.

Covenants bind the participants together. Covenants are thus more about relationship than the realization of an end, even a righteous end. The making and keeping of sacred covenants is all about linking an individual and a people to the Father and the Son.

In the first chapter of the book of Isaiah, Jehovah speaks painfully about the children of Israel: "Hear, O heavens, and give ear, O earth: for the Lord hath spoken, I have nourished and brought up children, and they have rebelled against me. The ox knoweth his owner, and the ass his master's crib [stall or manger]: but Israel doth not know, my people doth not consider" (Isaiah 1:2–3).

Similarly, Jehovah spoke through the prophet Hosea: "Hear the word of the Lord, ye children of Israel: for the Lord hath a controversy with the inhabitants of the land, because there is no truth, nor mercy, nor knowledge of God in the land" (Hosea 4:1). The Lord continues: "My people are destroyed for lack of knowledge: because thou hast rejected knowledge, I will also reject thee" (Hosea 4:6).

It was not that the children of Israel did not know about Jehovah—who he was, what he had done for them in the past, how he had interacted with Abraham and Moses. Surely most of Israel's descendants could have listed many qualities and attributes of the God of Abraham, Isaac, and Jacob. Certainly they could have had a worthwhile conversation about the Supreme Being. But they did not know him.

The word *know* that is used here does not refer to cognitive understanding, to so-called head knowledge. The Hebrew word translated as *know* denotes a deeper kind of knowledge, a knowledge of the heart, an experiential knowledge. Interestingly, it is the same word used early in the Bible when Moses explained that "Adam knew Eve his wife; and she conceived, and bare Cain" (Genesis 4:1). It is close, tender, intimate knowledge. In other words, when Jehovah laments that his people do not know him, he is proclaiming that the children of Israel do not enjoy the kind of close, tender, loving and committed association that God should enjoy with his chosen people. That is, Israel at that point in their history did not have a covenant knowledge of and love for their God. They did not enjoy the kind of intimate relationship that a covenant people could and should enjoy with Deity.

Covenant-making goes back a long time before our first parents were placed in Eden, even before the foundations of this earth were laid. On the very last page of the Book of Mormon, Moroni brings the magnificent Nephite-Jaredite record to a close by inviting its readers to "come unto Christ and be perfected in him, and deny yourselves of all ungodliness; and if ye shall deny yourselves of all ungodliness, and love God with all your might, mind, and strength, then is his grace sufficient for you, that by his grace ye may be perfect in Christ" (Moroni 10:32).

There it is—the eternal mission of the Church of Jesus Christ (compare D&C 20:59), the invitation to all humankind to come unto the Holy Messiah and enjoy perfection: wholeness, maturity, or completion in him. Or, as we are instructed in a modern revelation concerning those who inherit the highest degree of glory hereafter, "these are they who are just men made perfect through Jesus the mediator of the new covenant, who wrought out this perfect atonement through the shedding of his own blood" (D&C 76:69; compare Hebrews 13:20–21).

Moroni continues: "And again, if ye by the grace of God are perfect in Christ, and deny not his power, then are ye sanctified in Christ by the grace of God, *through the shedding of the blood of Christ, which is in the covenant of the Father unto the remission of your sins,* that ye become holy, without spot" (Moroni 10:33; emphasis added). That is a deep and insightful passage.

The Prophet Joseph Smith taught further: "Everlasting covenant was made between three personages before the organization of this earth and relates to their dispensation of things to men on the earth. These personages . . . are called

God the first, the Creator; God the second, the Redeemer; and God the third, the Witness or Testator" (*Joseph Smith,* 42).

President John Taylor explained that "a covenant was entered into between [Christ] and His Father, in which He agreed to atone for the sins of the world; and He thus . . . became the Lamb slain from before the foundation of the world." President Taylor also explained that through offering himself as a willing sacrifice for the sins of God's children, "the Savior thus becomes master of the situation—the debt is paid, the redemption made, *the covenant fulfilled,* justice satisfied, the will of God done, and all power is now given into the hands of the Son of God—the power of the resurrection, the power of the redemption, the power of salvation, the power to enact laws for the carrying out and accomplishment of this design" (*Mediation and Atonement,* 97, 171; emphasis added).

We too made covenants in our premortal existence. "I believe that when you and I were in yonder life," President Lorenzo Snow taught, "we made certain covenants with those that had the control, that in this life, when we should be permitted to enter it, we would do what we had done in that [premortal] life—find out the will of God and conform to it" (*Teachings of Lorenzo Snow,* 118–19). Elder John A. Widtsoe pointed out that in our first estate we "agreed, right then and there, to be not only saviors for ourselves, but . . . saviors for the whole human family. We went into a partnership with the Lord. The working out of the plan became then not merely the Father's work, and the Savior's work, but also our work. The least of us, the humblest, is in partnership with the Almighty in achieving the purpose of the eternal plan of salvation" (*Utah Genealogical and Historical Magazine,* October 1934, 189).

And so it has been through the ages. God covenanted with Enoch that he would never again flood the earth, and he confirmed that covenant with Noah (see Moses 7:50–51, 60; JST Genesis 9:21–25). Jehovah entered into covenant with Abraham, and the fulness of the gospel covenant which he made with the father of the faithful is so clearly spelled out in the book of Genesis (see Genesis 13:14–17; 15:1–10; 17:1–8) that we know it as the Abrahamic covenant.

The clearest statement of this covenant is found in the book of Abraham. There we learn that Jehovah expected Abraham's descendants to choose him as their God and to remain loyal to the royal within them. In return, Abraham's children were promised the gospel of Jesus Christ, the priesthood, and eternal lives, the perpetuation of the family in and beyond this life (see Abraham 2:8–11).

Following the deaths of the apostles in the meridian dispensation and the loss of the keys of the priesthood, the gospel covenant was no longer in effect in the Old World. Isaiah had described such a time: "The earth also is defiled under the inhabitants thereof; because they have transgressed the laws, changed the ordinance, broken the everlasting covenant" (Isaiah 24:5). Thus the Choice Seer charged to oversee the Restoration was destined to restore plain and precious truths that had been lost from the Bible through the centuries "and also many covenants of the Lord" (1 Nephi 13:26; see also vv. 28, 35–36).

In other words, the Restoration would consist of

"making known of the covenants of the Father of heaven unto Abraham, saying: In thy seed shall all the kindreds of the earth be blessed. . . . Wherefore, the Lord God will proceed to make bare his arm in the eyes of all the nations, *in bringing about his covenants and his gospel unto those who are of the house of Israel*" (1 Nephi 22:10–11; emphasis added). The restoration of the gospel that began with the appearance of the Father and the Son to the boy prophet in 1820 was in fact the restoration of the new and everlasting covenant—the restoration of the fulness of all laws and statutes and covenants required for salvation in the last days (see D&C 1:22; 45:9; 49:9; 66:2; 133:57; Smith, *Doctrines of Salvation,* 1:156).

In a letter to newspaper editor N. E. Seaton, the Prophet Joseph declared: "The time has at last arrived when the God of Abraham, of Isaac, and of Jacob, has set His hand again the second time to recover the remnants of His people. . . . This covenant has never been established with the house of Israel, nor with the house of Judah, for it requires two parties to make a covenant, and those two parties must be agreed, or no covenant can be made.

"Christ, in the days of His flesh, proposed to make a covenant with them, but they rejected Him and His proposals, and in consequence thereof, they were broken off, and no covenant was made with them at that time. But their unbelief has not rendered the promise of God of none effect; no, for there was another day . . . which was the day of His power; and then His people, Israel, should be a willing people."

The Prophet then called upon the inhabitants of the earth to "repent of all your sins, and be baptized in water for the remission of them, in the name of the Father, and of the Son, and of the Holy Ghost, and receive the ordinance of the laying on of the hands of him who is ordained and sealed unto this power, that ye may receive the Holy Spirit of God. . . . These are the requirements of the new covenant, or first principles of the Gospel of Christ" (*Joseph Smith*, 154).

In the Wentworth letter, Joseph explained that Moroni had been "sent to bring the joyful tidings that *the covenant which God made with ancient Israel was at hand to be fulfilled,* that the preparatory work for the second coming of the Messiah was speedily to commence, that the time was at hand for the Gospel in all its fullness to be preached in power, unto all nations that a people might be prepared for the Millennial reign. I was informed that I was chosen to be an instrument in the hands of God to bring about some of His purposes in this glorious dispensation" (*Joseph Smith*, 439; emphasis added).

It is easy in our busy and complex world to be distracted from the truth that the gospel of Jesus Christ is a gospel covenant and that we are a part of the outworking of a grand covenant made between God and Abraham and Abraham's descendants. In the thirty years that I worked as a professor of ancient scripture at Brigham Young University, it was my privilege to associate with some of the greatest young people in the Church's history, a body of believers who have been sent to the earth at a specific time for specific purposes and to engage specific challenges. They are indeed a generation of greatness. And yet there were those disappointing moments, here and there, when I sensed that a few of these wonderful Latter-day Saints had lost track, at least temporarily, of who they are—not as a son or daughter of God but as a child of Abraham, one in whose veins flows the blood of a royal lineage, one sent to earth with a redemptive mission, a mission to raise the sights of earth's inhabitants and lift the quality of life among mortals. That is, they seemed to have been lacking a sense of covenant consciousness, an inner awareness that in order to make a difference they needed to be different and to stand out from the crowd.

In our day the Savior has taught, "When men are called unto mine everlasting gospel, and covenant with an everlasting covenant, they are accounted as the salt of the earth and the savor of men; they are called to be the savor of men; therefore, if that salt of the earth lose its savor, behold it is thenceforth good for nothing only to be cast out and trodden under the feet of men" (D&C 101:39–40). Or, stated another way, the men of the covenant—and for our purposes, the men of the priesthood—are given a redemptive role on earth: they are "set to be a light unto the world, and *to be the saviors of men*; and inasmuch as they are not the saviors of men, they are as salt that has lost its savor" (D&C 103:9–10; emphasis added).

In short, as Elder Russell M. Nelson pointed out, "When we know who we are and what God expects of us—when His 'law [is] written in our hearts'—we are spiritually protected. We become better people" (*Perfection Pending*, 193).

President Boyd K. Packer spoke of a man who seemed to have his heart and mind riveted on covenant. "Several years ago I installed a stake president in England. . . . He had an unusual sense of direction. He was like a mariner with a sextant who took his bearings from the stars. I met with him each time he came to [general] conference and was impressed that he kept himself and his stake on course.

"Fortunately for me, when it was time for his release, I was assigned to reorganize the stake. It was then that I discovered what that sextant was and how he adjusted it to check his position and get a bearing for himself and for his members.

"He accepted his release, and said: 'I was happy to accept the call to serve as stake president, and I am equally happy to accept my release. I did not serve just because I was under call. *I served because I am under covenant.* And I can keep my covenants quite as well as a home teacher as I can serving as stake president.'

"This president understood the word *covenant.*

"While he was neither a scriptorian nor a gospel scholar, he somehow had learned that *exaltation is achieved by keeping covenants,* not by holding high position" (*Ensign,* May 1987, 23–24; emphasis added).

We live in perilous times today. We are witnessing the secularization of our society, the gradual devolution of time-honored values and absolute truths, and the erosion of many of our precious liberties, including religious liberty. It will not be by military might nor intellectual genius that our world will be spared the tests and trials and calamities that lie ahead. Nor will the information explosion bring the kind of saving insights and perspectives on life that will result in a happy and pain-free world.

Nephi saw the solution in vision: "I, Nephi, beheld the power of the Lamb of God, that it descended upon the saints of the church of the Lamb, and *upon the covenant people of the Lord,* who were scattered upon all the face of the earth; and *they were armed with righteousness and with the power of God* in great glory" (1 Nephi 14:14; emphasis added).

We are a covenant-making people, a people who are striving to draw near to that Lord who is the Mediator of the everlasting covenant. "And this shall be our covenant—that we will walk in all the ordinances of the Lord" (D&C 136:4). Therein is safety. Therein is peace.

THE OATH AND COVENANT
OF THE PRIESTHOOD

SOME THREE YEARS AFTER the conferral of the Melchizedek Priesthood upon Joseph Smith and Oliver Cowdery, another covenant was revealed to the restored Church. In a revelation given through the Prophet in Kirtland, the Lord outlined what has come to be known as the Oath and Covenant of the Melchizedek Priesthood. Jesus Christ declared:

"For whoso is faithful unto the obtaining these two priesthoods of which I have spoken [Aaronic and Melchizedek], and the magnifying their calling, are sanctified by the Spirit unto the renewing of their bodies.

"They become the sons of Moses and of Aaron and the seed of Abraham, and the church and kingdom, and the elect of God.

"And also all they who receive this priesthood receive me, saith the Lord;

"For he that receiveth my servants receiveth me;

"And he that receiveth me receiveth my Father;

"And he that receiveth my Father receiveth my Father's

kingdom; therefore all that my Father hath shall be given unto him.

"And this is according to the oath and covenant which belongeth to the priesthood.

"Therefore, all those who receive the priesthood, receive this oath and covenant of my Father, which he cannot break, neither can it be moved.

"But whoso breaketh this covenant after he hath received it, and altogether turneth therefrom, shall not have forgiveness of sins in this world nor in the world to come.

"And wo unto all those who come not unto this priesthood which ye have received, which I now confirm upon you who are present this day, by mine own voice out of the heavens; and even I have given the heavenly hosts and mine angels charge concerning you.

"And now I give unto you a commandment to beware concerning yourselves, to give diligent heed to the words of eternal life.

"For you shall live by every word that proceedeth forth from the mouth of God" (D&C 84:33–44).

Let us be reminded that the priesthood is the power of God, delegated to man on earth, to act in all things for the salvation of humankind. Joseph Smith taught: "The priesthood is an everlasting principle, and existed with God from eternity, and will to eternity, without beginning of days or end of years" (*Joseph Smith,* 104). This priesthood "is the channel through which all knowledge, doctrine, the plan of salvation, and every important matter is revealed from heaven. . . . It is the channel through which the Almighty commenced revealing His glory at the beginning of the creation of this earth, and through which He has continued to reveal Himself to the children of men to the present time, and through which He will make known His purposes to the end of time" (*Joseph Smith,* 108–9).

Every recipient of the Melchizedek Priesthood enters into a covenant with God (see Hebrews 7:17, 21; *Joseph Smith,* 108–9). As we have seen, a covenant is a two-way promise: we promise God certain things, and God promises us certain things in return.

We Promise	God Promises
Obtain the priesthood	We are sanctified and renewed
Magnify callings in the priesthood	We become sons of Moses and Aaron
Receive the Lord's servants	We become the seed of Abraham
Beware concerning ourselves	
Give diligent heed to the words of eternal life	We enter the church and kingdom
Live by every word of God	We become the elect of God
	We receive Christ and the Father
	We receive all the Father has

In the chapters that follow, we will examine the specific commitments we make to God (which compose our part of the covenant) and then reflect on the blessings the Lord promises to bestow upon us if we keep the covenant.

I remember very well the small apartment in Greenfield, Massachusetts, that my companion and I lived in as full-time missionaries. One morning during personal study time, I stumbled across verses 33 through 44 of Doctrine and Covenants 84. I reread those verses a couple of times and found myself focusing on the phrase "all those who receive the priesthood receive this oath and covenant." *All those.* The language of the revelation seemed rather inclusive, suggesting that I was in that group. I read on and discovered that if I broke the covenant, I would not be forgiven here or hereafter.

Good grief! This was serious stuff! I then reflected on my interview with my priesthood leaders in my home stake some four or five months earlier. I certainly didn't remember hearing anything about how my being ordained an elder would cause me to enter into some kind of covenant with God that, if broken, would doom me forever. My initial feelings of terror were soon replaced by feelings of frustration, bordering on anger. Why hadn't anyone told me about this? Why hadn't this ever been discussed in Primary or Sunday School, or, especially, priesthood meeting? I had been instructed by wonderful quorum advisers, but somehow this topic had never come up.

As my companion and I knocked on doors throughout the day, I couldn't rid myself of the weight I felt on my shoulders as a result of reading a few verses of a modern revelation. As time passed, however, the anxiety began to lift, but I determined that I really needed to look into this matter more thoroughly. Missionary work and the focus on memorizing scriptures, learning the discussions, tracting, visiting

Church members in the area to obtain referrals, teaching investigators, and district and zone conferences consumed me and, providentially, distracted me for a season. After returning home from the mission and then attending school at Louisiana State University for another semester, I transferred to Brigham Young University.

At BYU I registered for a course in the second half of the Doctrine and Covenants, which at that time consisted of a study of sections 71–136. I am grateful that the professor chose to spend almost an entire fifty-minute period on section 84, particularly those twelve verses associated with the oath and covenant of the priesthood. I essentially sat on the edge of my chair when we came to the part about what would happen to us if we broke the covenant. The words "shall not have forgiveness of sins in this world nor in the world to come" (D&C 84:41) sounded really ominous—very similar, in fact, to the fate of the sons of perdition (see Matthew 12:31–32; D&C 76:31–35).

The professor then read to us the following from President Joseph Fielding Smith, at that time president of the Quorum of the Twelve Apostles: "Now when a man makes a covenant that he will receive the priesthood and magnify it, and then he violates that covenant, 'and altogether turneth therefrom'—there is a chance to repent if he does not altogether turn therefrom—then there is no 'forgiveness of sins in this world nor in the world to come.' That does *not* mean that man is going to become a son of perdition, but the meaning is that *he will never again have the opportunity of exercising the priesthood and receiving exaltation.* That is where his forgiveness ends. He will not again have the priesthood conferred upon him, because he has trampled it under his feet; but as far as other things are concerned, he may be forgiven" (*Doctrines of Salvation*, 3:141–42).

I wondered, not long after that class period, whether some men, coming face to face with the terrible consequences of breaking the covenant, might decide not to advance from the Aaronic to the Melchizedek Priesthood. They just might be prone to refuse ordination. Better to be safe than sorry. Right?

Later I read the following from President Marion G. Romney: "When I first began to seriously think about this statement [D&C 84:41], I wondered if it would not have been better for me never to have received the priesthood, if failing to magnify my callings in it would mean I would never receive forgiveness in this world nor in the world to come. As I pondered over this and the next verse, which reads, 'And *wo unto all those who come not unto this priesthood*' (D&C 84:42), I finally came to the conclusion that I was on the horns of a dilemma—that *my only hope was to receive the priesthood and magnify my callings in it*" (*Look to God and Live*, 55; emphasis added).

We know that there are two different ways to commit sin and thus dishonor the priesthood we bear. The first is the more obvious—by breaking the commandments, that is, by violating the standards set forth in scripture and as expanded upon by the Lord's anointed servants. John wrote: "Whosoever committeth sin transgresseth also the law: for sin is the transgression of the law" (1 John 3:4). The other way, and one that often escapes our notice, is to fail to do what we have been charged and called upon to do, that is, to be guilty of sins of omission. James, the brother of our Lord and Savior, put it simply: "Therefore to him that knoweth to do good, and doeth it not, to him it is sin" (James 4:17). President Spencer W. Kimball observed that "one breaks the priesthood covenant by transgressing commandments—but also by leaving undone his duties. Accordingly, to break this covenant one needs only do nothing" (*Teachings of Spencer W. Kimball*, 497). Thus the men of the priesthood must guard against falling into sin, but we must also guard against falling into laziness or indifference. Either way, we have opened ourselves to Satan's power and denied ourselves access to the power of the Savior.

Let's consider now what an oath is. Anciently individuals relied on an oath as an outward witness of the truth of some fact or matter. The oath represented a solemn attestation, and "to swear with an oath [was] the most solemn and binding form of speech known to the human tongue" (Smith, Conference Report, April 1970, 92). The power of an oath in antiquity is seen in the fact that, in Nephi's words, "when Zoram had made an oath unto us, our fears did cease concerning him" (1 Nephi 4:37). Further, in antiquity even bad guys did not swear oaths they knew they would break (see Alma 44:8).

The wicked use of the oath to bring about unholy ends began early in man's history. Cain swore unto Satan by an oath that he would not reveal the nature of the "great secret"—namely, that there was advantage to be gained in wanton murder (Moses 5:31). From these beginnings have come the myriads of secret combinations, bound by unholy oaths, in which the wicked have vowed to destroy the works of God.

In his magnificent Sermon on the Mount, the Savior called his people to better things:

"Again, ye have heard that it hath been said by them of old time, Thou shalt not foreswear thyself [break your oaths], but shalt perform unto the Lord thy oaths [see Leviticus 19:22].

"But I say unto you, Swear not at all; neither by heaven; for it is God's throne:

"Nor by the earth; for it is his footstool; neither by Jerusalem; for it is the city of the great King.

"Neither shall thou swear by thy head, because thou canst not make one hair white or black.

"But let your communication be Yea, yea; Nay, nay; for whatsoever is more than these cometh of evil" (Matthew 5:33–37).

Here was a call to a higher righteousness. Man was no longer to swear by anything—his word was to be his bond; yes or no was sufficient. Under the law of Moses, there was always the possibility that a man might not keep his promises unless he swore by an oath to keep them (see Numbers 30:2). Under the law of Christ, man was deemed to be trustworthy enough, possessed of sufficient integrity that oaths were no longer necessary.

What's the difference, then, between the oath and the covenant, as it pertains to the Melchizedek Priesthood? To be sure, there are times when these two words are used interchangeably in the scriptures (see Mosiah 5:5; 6:3). But in the case of the oath and covenant of the priesthood, they are not the same. The covenant consists of what we promise God and what he promises us, as those terms are spelled out in Doctrine and Covenants 84:33–44. But the oath is another thing entirely. "There is an oath and covenant of the priesthood," President Boyd K. Packer explained. "The covenant rests with man; the oath with God. The Melchizedek Priesthood is received by covenant. A man's covenant with God is: to be faithful and magnify his callings in the priesthood; to give heed to the words of eternal life; and to live by every word that proceedeth forth from the mouth of God" (*Ensign,* February 1993, 9–10; see also D&C 84:33, 43–44).

President Ezra Taft Benson distilled the matter in this way: "When a priesthood holder takes upon himself the Melchizedek Priesthood, he does so by oath and covenant. This is not so with the Aaronic Priesthood. The covenant of the Melchizedek Priesthood is that a priesthood holder will magnify his calling in the priesthood, will give diligent heed to the commandments of God, and will live by every word which proceeds 'from the mouth of God' (see D&C 84:33–44). The oath of the Melchizedek Priesthood is an irrevocable promise by God to faithful priesthood holders. 'All that my Father hath shall be given unto them' (see D&C 84:38). This oath by Deity, coupled with the covenant by faithful priesthood holders, is referred to as the oath and covenant of the priesthood" (*Teachings of Ezra Taft Benson,* 223).

We would suppose that this is the same oath sworn by God to Enoch and Melchizedek (see JST Genesis 14:25–40) as well as to Nephi, son of Helaman (see Helaman 10:1–7), the same oath sworn to all former-day Saints who were true and faithful to their covenants.

We are under covenant. We are men under covenant. Having received the Melchizedek Priesthood, we have taken upon ourselves an incomparable responsibility that is inextricably linked to an incomparable blessing. Given all that God has promised to those who are true and faithful to the covenant, those who "walk in the light, as [Christ] is in the light" (1 John 1:7), is it any wonder that our Lord and God expects serious dedication from us? Given that our faithfulness to the covenant will exert a righteous influence that will affect how we and our posterity spend eternity, is it any wonder that Deity has placed sobering responsibilities on our shoulders? (see Eyring, *Ensign,* May 2014, 22).

We can accept those responsibilities or refuse them. The choice is ours.

POINTS TO PONDER

1. When does a person become a "covenant person"?

2. What is the difference between a genuine commitment and a gospel covenant?

3. In the oath and covenant of the Melchizedek Priesthood, what is the oath and who swears it? What is promised?

4. In the oath and covenant of the Melchizedek Priesthood, what is the covenant and who enters into it? What is promised?

OBTAIN THE PRIESTHOOD

SOME TIME AGO I SAT IN AN AIRPLANE flying from Ontario, California, to Salt Lake City. It was a trip that would occupy a little less than two hours. But I had a great deal on my mind, much to accomplish in the next few days, and too little time to get it done. I found myself plotting how I would pull it off, what hours of what day in the coming week I could devote specifically to meeting the deadlines. As I was staring at my appointment book and just as I was making some calculations and time commitment, the man in the seat next to me chose to strike up a conversation.

"How are you?" he asked.

I nodded and offered a perfunctory smile.

I was trying once more to focus on my burdens when he spoke again.

"Do you live in Salt Lake? Are you traveling home?"

I offered extremely brief responses and tried to indicate without words that I had important things to do.

But my seatmate would have none of it. "What do you do for a living?" he inquired.

I told him I was a professor.

"What kind of a professor are you?" he came right back. "What do you teach?"

I explained that I was a professor of religion at Brigham Young University, and, to my chagrin, he got even more interested in conversing with me.

"Wow, that's pretty cool," he said. "What kind of religion do you teach? Do you just teach Mormon stuff?"

Hesitantly and painfully I replied that while I did in fact teach Latter-day Saint scripture and doctrine, I also taught New Testament and spent much of my time working with persons of other Christian faiths.

That was a real mistake. My fascinated friend then invited me to go into detail about what kinds of dialogues and meetings and conferences I had been a part of for the past twenty years. I tried to answer the man's questions thoroughly but also briefly enough that we could soon end this encounter.

He finally gave up, smiled, and wished me well.

In the hours and days that followed that flight, I found myself languishing in guilt over a missed opportunity. A missionary moment had dropped into my lap, and I had blown it by choosing to focus on things of lesser worth and to be emotionally and spiritually inaccessible to this inquirer.

The other thought that plagued me—and still haunts me to this day—is that there are probably few coincidences when it comes to when we encounter whom we encounter on this earth. For all I know, this particular setting, one hundred minutes essentially alone with this specific son of God, was orchestrated by a higher power. And I was simply too caught up with myself, too obsessed with my to-do list, to recognize this meeting for what it was. Would he have been open to the message of the Restoration? Would he have accepted that message, come into the Church, and become a great contributor to the work of the kingdom of God? Even if he was not inclined to change faiths and be baptized, could I have given to him some understanding about Latter-day Saints, our beliefs and way of life, that would make a difference down the road? This is a story of what might have been.

Because I believe there are very few coincidences in life, I also believe that we are not where we are by chance or happenstance. I feel confident that we are where we are because there are things we can do with people who are here that no one else can do in quite the same way. There are likely very few accidents, at least in our association with the sons and daughters of our Eternal Father. And that would also be true for each of us as holders of God's holy priesthood. We are told in the revelation that we are expected, first of all, to obtain the priesthood. That sounds simple enough, doesn't it? And yet, surely God has not left to chance who obtains and receives his sacred authority, especially given the redemptive labor we are charged to undertake.

What are the odds that you or I would hold the priesthood? If we consider that there are roughly seven billion people on earth, fifteen million of whom are Latter-day Saints, with about half that number being active and participating and less than half that number who have received the Melchizedek Priesthood, what are the odds of being ordained an elder or a high priest? Pretty small.

I remember when the president of the Church announced to the Saints that Church membership had passed fifteen million. I was impressed, mainly because I happen to know that in 1947, the year I was born, Church membership reached the one million mark. But whenever I get a little cocky about our growth and our influence in the world, I am brought up short by the realization that today there are approximately 1.2 billion Roman Catholics, 1.3 billion Muslims, somewhere in the neighborhood of 250 million members of Eastern Orthodox faiths, and about 300 million to 500 million Evangelical Protestants. And that's not even considering how many Hindus, Buddhists, or participants in other eastern religions there are throughout the world. Humbling, isn't it? Obviously we have a great deal of work to do before the Good Ship Zion can dock in her harbor.

Just as it is inconceivable that one person is tabernacled in the flesh at a given place and in a given time by chance alone, so when it came to the organization of humankind into lineages and families, nothing was left to chance. Our Father in Heaven is a God of order, and his house is a house of order. There is purpose and design in all he seeks to do, in all he seeks to bring to pass. The Prophet Joseph Smith taught that the sons and daughters of God were organized in our premortal existence (see *Joseph Smith*, 104; *Words of Joseph Smith*, 60).

This teaching is borne out in a translation of an ancient text: "Now the Lord had shown unto me, Abraham, the intelligences that were organized before the world was; and among all these there were many of the noble and great ones" (Abraham 3:22). This organization refers to the calling or assignment of individuals to certain blessings and responsibilities in the second estate.

After his death, the Prophet Joseph appeared to Brigham Young and pleaded: "Tell the people to be humble and faithful, and be sure to keep the Spirit of the Lord and it will lead them right. . . . Tell the brethren if they will follow the Spirit of the Lord, they will go right. Be sure to tell the people to keep the Spirit of the Lord; and if they will they will find themselves just as they were organized by our Father in Heaven before they came into the world. Our Father in Heaven organized the human family, but they are [now] all disorganized and in great confusion" (*Joseph Smith*, 98; Journal History, 23 February 1847).

Following our birth as spirit sons and daughters of God and being endowed with agency, we grew and developed and progressed according to our desires for truth and righteousness. It is customary to remark that in our first estate we walked by sight, while in this life we walk by faith. This is only partially true. In that previous existence we walked by sight and we also walked by faith. The scriptures teach that some exercised exceedingly great faith and performed many good works (see Alma 13:3). That the Lord should state that many were among the noble and great ones certainly implies a gradation of faithfulness, that some were less noble and some even ignoble.

Though often Saints may be inclined to speak of

individual foreordination to priesthood positions, callings, or assignments in the Church, perhaps the greatest fore-ordination or election based on premortal faithfulness is foreordination to lineage. Individuals come to earth through a designated lineage that entitles them to specified blessings, a lineage that carries with it responsibilities. This is what my colleague Brent Top calls "a type of collective foreordina-tion—a selection of spirits to form an entire favored group or lineage." Yet, he observes, "although it is a collective fore-ordination, it is nonetheless based on individual premortal faithfulness and spiritual capacity" (*Life Before,* 144).

In the words of Elder Melvin J. Ballard, Israel is "a group of souls tested, tried, and proven before they were born into the world. . . . Through this lineage were to come the true and tried souls that had demonstrated their righteousness in the spirit world before they came here" (*Crusader for Righteousness,* 218–19).

"Remember the days of old," Moses counseled his people, "consider the years of many generations: ask thy father, and he will shew thee: thy elders, and they will tell thee. When the most High divided to the nations their inheritance, when he separated the sons of Adam, *he set the bounds of the people according to the number of the children of Israel.* For the Lord's portion is his people; Jacob is the lot of his inheritance" (Deuteronomy 32:7–9; emphasis added).

In speaking to the Athenians, the apostle Paul declared: "God that made the world and all things therein . . . hath made of one blood all nations of men for to dwell on all the face of the earth, and *hath determined the times before appointed, and the bounds of their habitation*" (Acts 17:24–26; emphasis added).

President Harold B. Lee explained that "those born to the lineage of Jacob, who was later to be called Israel, and his posterity, who were known as the children of Israel, were born into the most illustrious lineage of any of those who came upon the earth as mortal beings. All these rewards were seemingly promised, or foreordained, before the world was. Surely these matters must have been determined by the kind of lives we had lived in that premortal spirit world. Some may question these assumptions, but at the same time they will accept without any question the belief that each one of us will be judged when we leave this earth according to his or her deeds during our lives here in mortality. Isn't it just as reasonable to believe that what we have received here in this earth [life] was given to each of us according to the merits of our conduct before we came here?" (*Ensign*, January 1974, 5). Thus the declaration of our lineage by patriarchs is as much a statement about who and what we were as it is about who we are now and what we may become.

Again, it is no accident that you and I have obtained the priesthood. Indeed, the Prophet Joseph Smith taught that "every man who has a calling to minister to the inhabitants of the world"—and that certainly refers to holders of the Melchizedek Priesthood—"was ordained to that very purpose in the Grand Council of heaven before this world was. I suppose," the Prophet meekly commented, "I was ordained to this very office in that Grand Council" (*Joseph Smith*, 511). Yes, I suppose he was!

In speaking of those who were foreordained to receive the high priesthood, Alma explained that they were "called and prepared from the foundation of the world according to the foreknowledge of God, on account of their exceeding faith and good works [in the premortal life]; in the first place [in that first estate] being left to choose good or evil; therefore they having chosen good, and exercising exceedingly great faith, are called [in this life] with a holy calling, yea, with that holy calling which was prepared with, and according to, a preparatory redemption for such" (Alma 13:3).

Making sense of that one verse is not easy. While this language may seem a little odd, I do get a sense of Alma's meaning. Many years ago my friend and colleague Joseph Fielding McConkie and I made the following comment on this verse: "All doctrines, ordinances, and powers associated with the gospel of Jesus Christ assume force and meaning only in and through Christ's atoning sacrifice. Such was the plan prepared before the foundation of the earth. Men are called to receive the priesthood to assist in the redemption of souls. They are called to preach and make available what Paul described as the 'ministry of reconciliation' (2 Corinthians 5:18). They are called to bless lives—to lighten burdens, strengthen the feeble knees, and lift up the hands that hang down (see D&C 81:5)—just as their Master, the Great High Priest, is called upon to do. The priesthood bearers before and after Christ are thus involved in the work of his ministry. Their work is preparatory. They, like the preeminent forerunner, John the Baptist, prepare the way of the Lord. Those prophets and priests who labored before the meridian of time sought to prepare mankind for the coming of the Redeemer. . . . Those who have lived since that time seek to instruct and warn and exhort mankind—all in preparation for his second advent, that final redemption of the earth and its inhabitants" (*Doctrinal Commentary on the Book of Mormon,* 3:95).

And so, we have been faithful in that we have obtained the priesthood. We have fulfilled the first condition of the covenant of the priesthood. We are indeed a blessed people. But what if you or I had lived three or four hundred years ago? I reflect with profound soberness that there was then no one on earth with authority to confer the priesthood and no one holding the keys to ensure the proper performance of the ordinances. The Prophet Joseph Smith remarked that "a man can do nothing for himself unless God direct him in the right way; and the priesthood is for that purpose" (*Joseph Smith,* 109). The priesthood is a power no man can assume, take upon himself, or even purchase; it comes through the laying on of hands by those holding proper authority (see Acts 8:18–20; Hebrews 5:4).

Perhaps it would help us appreciate what we have available to us and within our grasp, what it means to have been ordained by one having sacred authority, by considering what our lives might have been like if we had lived three hundred years ago, at a time and in a day when the power and authority of God was not to be found on earth. Latter-day Saints believe that with the death of the apostles and within one hundred years of the crucifixion of Jesus, this authority and power to act in the name of God was lost from the earth. Hegesippus, the second-century Jewish-Christian writer, noted that "when the sacred band of the apostles had in various ways reached the end of their life, and the generation of those privileged to listen with their own ears to the divine wisdom had passed on, then godless error began to take shape" (Eusebius, *History of the Church*, 96).

Similarly, biblical scholar J. B. Phillips observed that the differences between present-day traditional Christianity and the young church of the first century A.D. are readily apparent. The early Christians "did not make 'acts of faith,' they believed; they did not 'say their prayers,' they really prayed. They did not hold conferences on psychosomatic medicine, they simply healed the sick. . . . We in the modern Church have unquestionably *lost* something. Whether it is due to the atrophy of the quality which the New Testament calls 'faith,' whether it is due to a stifling churchiness, whether it is due to our sinful complacency over the scandal of a divided Church, or whatever the cause may be, very little of the modern Church could bear comparison with the spiritual drive, the genuine fellowship, and the gay [i.e., joyful] unconquerable courage of the Young Church" (*The Young Church in Action*, 11, 20–21, as cited in Morrison, *Turning from the Truth*, 51–52).

The story is told that on one occasion the pope "pointed to his gorgeous Papal Palace and said [to St. Dominic], 'Peter can no longer say 'Silver and gold have I none''; and the Spanish friar answered, 'No, and neither can he now say, 'Rise and walk'" (in Chesterton, *St. Thomas Acquinas*, 34–35).

While both Roman Catholic and Orthodox Christians claim apostolic succession—meaning that the bishops of the ancient church have conveyed their priesthood powers down to the pope and patriarch in our time—we as Latter-day Saints teach that God's divine authority was not to be found in the Old World by the middle of the second century A.D. Other than the formal break between western (Roman) and eastern (Orthodox) Christianity in A.D. 1054, the Roman church had control of the Christian faith until the sixteenth century, when courageous men and women objected to, opposed, and broke away from Catholicism.

Again from the Prophet Joseph: "It is in the order of heavenly things that God should always send a new dispensation into the world when men have apostatized from the truth and lost the priesthood. . . . [But] when men come out and build upon other men's foundations, they do it on their own responsibility, without authority from God" (*Joseph Smith,* 510, 523).

Late in his life, Roger Williams renounced the views of the Baptists and "turned seeker, i.e., to wait for new apostles to restore Christianity." He felt the need "of a special commission, to restore the modes of positive worship, according to the original institution." Williams concluded that the Protestants were "not . . . able to derive the authority . . . from the apostles, . . . [and] conceived God would raise up some apostolic power" (in Backman, *American Religions,* 180–81; see also Holland, *Ensign,* November 2004, 7–8).

In short, Williams held that there was "no regularly constituted church of Christ, on earth, nor any person authorized to administer any church ordinance, nor can there be until new apostles are sent by the great head of the Church, for whose coming, I am seeking" (in Richards, *Marvelous Work and a Wonder,* 25).

John Wesley was a marvelous preacher and religious leader in the eighteenth century and became essentially the father of Methodism. In speaking of him, Brigham Young observed: "I never passed John Wesley's church in London without stopping to look at it. Was he a good man? Yes; I suppose him to have been by all accounts, as good as ever walked on this earth, according to his knowledge. Has he obtained a rest? Yes, and greater than ever entered his mind to expect; and so have thousands of others of the various religious denominations. *Why could he not build up the Kingdom of God on the earth? He had not the Priesthood;* that was all the difficulty he labored under. Had the Priesthood been conferred upon him, he would have built up the Kingdom of God in his day as it is now being built up. He would have introduced the ordinances, powers, grades, and quorums of the Priesthood; but, not holding the Priesthood, he could not do it" (*Journal of Discourses,* 7:5; emphasis added).

John's brother Charles is responsible for many magnificent hymns sung in Christianity today. Though they were very close as brothers, on one occasion Charles criticized John when the latter ordained a man to an office without authority to do so. Charles wrote:

> How easily are bishops made
> By man or woman's whim:
> Wesley his hands on Coke hath laid,
> But who laid hands on him?
> (in Holland, *Ensign,* May 2005, 44)

Finally, I say once again, it is no accident that we as Latter-day Saints have received the priesthood of God. It is part of a grand plan of salvation, a plan that includes the Father's marvelous and mysterious orchestrations of people and events, all so that the greatest number of persons might be blessed with the fulness of the gospel and the grandest and highest privileges of the holy priesthood attainable. In speaking of his own role in reestablishing the fulness of priesthood blessings on the earth, Joseph Smith said: "Inasmuch as the Lord Almighty has preserved me until today, He will continue to preserve me, by the united faith and prayers of the Saints, until I have fully accomplished my mission in this life, and so firmly established the dispensation of the fullness of the priesthood in the last days, that all the powers of earth and hell can never prevail against it" (*Joseph Smith*, 531).

No one was foreordained to be a failure; no one was promised in that first estate that they would one day inherit the terrestrial kingdom; no one was sent to earth who did not have the capacity to eventually inherit the highest degree of the celestial kingdom. We have been ordained to greatness. A spiritually hungry and somewhat frightened world needs us to rise up and conduct ourselves as men of God.

POINTS TO PONDER

1. What does it mean to be foreordained? What does it not mean?

2. What difference does it make to you to know that you were foreordained?

3. What are the odds that you, a Latter-day Saint living in today's world, would be chosen to bear God's holy priesthood? What does that understanding do for you?

4. How is it that priesthood holders are to become "a light unto the world, and to be the saviors of men"? (D&C 103:9). To what extent are we given a redemptive role?

MAGNIFY OUR CALLINGS

JUST ABOUT ONE YEAR BEFORE LEAVING on a full-time mission, I was called to serve as a home teaching companion to a rather recent convert to the Church. He and his family had been pillars in the Presbyterian church in our small Louisiana community but had come in contact with the local missionaries, heard the message of the restored gospel, and received it. We were told that two of the families we were to visit lived many miles to the north and that they had not been active in the Church for many years.

My companion, Brother Coleman McVea Sr., was a recently ordained elder, and I was a priest, a bearer of the Aaronic Priesthood. Brother McVea received this calling with enthusiasm and resolve, and my first meeting with him seemed stunningly similar to a high school pep rally. On the first Tuesday of each month we met at my companion's home at 6:00 P.M. There we chatted briefly about the families and what we hoped to accomplish in our visit. Then we would pray. And boy, did this man know how to

37

pray! I had encountered very few people at that stage of my young life who prayed with the depth of sincerity and single-mindedness that he did. There was a pleading, a yearning in his voice that I now realize came from the depths of his soul, a Christlike love and tender regard for people whom he barely knew.

We followed the same pattern the first Tuesday of every month. Both families agreed begrudgingly on a time when we could meet regularly: the first family at 7:00, the second at 7:30. The composition of each family was very different, but they did have one thing in common: they did not want us to be there. At our first several meetings we would ring the doorbell of the first family precisely at 7:00, and either the husband or the wife would answer the door, roll their eyes as they realized that we were back, turn around, and head back into the family room, barely managing the words "Come on in." We would walk in, take a seat, and attempt to communicate with them, which was tough, since they never felt inclined to turn off the television. They only occasionally looked in our direction, and it seemed to me at the time that they had little concern for the brief gospel message we managed to leave. This went on month after month.

Each month, in our preparatory meeting and prayer session at my companion's home, I would say something like the following: "Why are we doing this? Why are we wasting our time? These people don't want us in their homes, and they couldn't care less about the gospel. Let's ask the bishop to assign us to some folks who really want us to visit them." My wise and sweet companion—almost fifty years later, I am in tears as I think about him, now deceased—Brother McVea would tenderly and patiently say to me, "Now, Robert, these good people need us. They need the gospel, as much as my family needed it. We owe it to them to do everything in our power to see that they receive it. They just don't realize now how badly they need what only you and I have to give them. Besides all that, the bishop assigned us to be their home teachers, and that assignment had to come by revelation. The Lord knows what he's doing."

I am embarrassed now as I recall painfully what I thought and felt when Brother McVea made those kinds of comments. I remember thinking, "He's a rookie in the Church. What does he know? I've been home teaching for four years now, and I know when people don't care. He is so naïve." But we met together, prayed together, traveled together, and knocked on those two doors together, month in and month out. The people could set their clocks by our knock on the door. I adjusted gradually to our assignment, especially when I realized that my companion was bound and determined to do his duty. And, I have to admit, as the months passed, the people we met with became more friendly, more welcoming, more cordial, and managed to turn off the TV when we entered their homes. I even recall our having a pretty good gospel discussion one evening about the doctrine of eternal families. By December of that year things were moving forward with my mission preparation, and by the first part of the year I left for the Eastern States Mission.

I had never been away from my family for longer than a week (scout camp), and so in the first few months I experienced, as do many of our missionaries, a brief season of homesickness. The thought that I might desert the mission and return home early never crossed my mind, but I did miss my parents, siblings, and grandparents very much. What made life away from home much more manageable was my family's encouraging and inspiring letters. I found letters from Mom and my grandmother in my mailbox every week. Dad, on the other hand, wrote to me about every other month. He would share how the work of the Lord was going forward in the New Orleans Stake, the unit to which our ward was attached, even though we were some seventy miles away from New Orleans itself. He spoke of his assignment as bishop and later of his duties as a high councilor, and I can sense now that he was providing for me a strong foundation in priesthood and Church government. Dad was an amazing leader in the Church, a man who accomplished so much but who also loved the people he served, and I have never forgotten his example.

The other letters that I received quite regularly, epistles that really stirred my soul, were from my former home teaching companion, Brother McVea. He spoke of the progress our home teaching families were making, and as the months passed he would inform me of children's baptisms, the families' attendance at church, and their acceptance of callings and assignments. And then, to my sheer and unexpected delight, he began writing of their preparation to attend the temple and be sealed eternally as a family. I remember having mixed feelings, a blend of joy and remorse of conscience, as odd a combination as those two are. Of course it was thrilling to learn that these people had truly grown in the gospel and progressed to the point that they were now about to receive the highest and holiest of ordinances a family can receive. At the same time I felt chastened for my youthful shortsightedness, for what was obviously a lack of faith, a reluctance to accept that what we were doing as home teachers was meaningful and worthwhile, that it had long-range consequences, and that it was just what the Savior would have us do. Our Master "went about doing good, . . . for God was with him" (Acts 10:38). Humbly I had to acknowledge that as a companionship of home teachers, we had indeed gone about doing good, that God had been with us, and that these sweet families had been the beneficiaries of Brother McVea's quiet but persistent ministry.

We are told in the revelation that sets forth the terms and conditions of the oath and covenant of the Melchizedek Priesthood that after we have obtained the priesthood, we are to magnify our callings within and under the direction of that priesthood (see D&C 84:33). President Joseph Fielding Smith taught: "Sometimes we speak loosely of magnifying our priesthood, but what the revelations speak of is *magnifying our callings in the priesthood* as elders, seventies, high priests, patriarchs, and apostles" (Conference Report, October 1970, 91–92; emphasis added).

So what does it mean to magnify a calling? How had Brother McVea magnified his calling as a new convert and a recently assigned home teacher?

First, he accepted his assignment from the bishop and the elders quorum president. No one had to tell Brother

McVea just how inexperienced, lacking in Church sense, and even deficient in gospel understanding he was. He knew those things only too well. But he had been called of God, and he knew it. Consequently he acted—he moved forward with faith—and in time the Almighty rewarded that faith.

Second, he did his duty with consistency. Month in and month out, he knocked on the first door at 7:00 P.M. Those families knew he would be there, his Church leaders knew he would be there, and our Father in Heaven knew he would be there—at his duty station, carrying out his sacred responsibility. His was a simple faith that if he moved forward to accomplish his task or calling, positive results would follow. People's hearts would be touched. The less active would be fully activated.

Third, and perhaps most important, Brother McVea loved the people he served, and they knew it. It may have taken them several months to recognize divine love in his eyes and in the tone of his voice, but they soon began to pick up on the fact that this guy was for real. He was genuinely on the Lord's errand.

It won't surprise you if I say that this simple home teaching experience with Brother McVea changed my life. I have never been the same since late 1966. I have been a home teacher since my return from the mission, and when I have been a bit lazy about making appointments early in the month; a bit shy in carrying out my duty to "watch over the church always, and be with and strengthen them"; somewhat hesitant to "see that there is no iniquity in the church, neither hardness with each other, neither lying, backbiting, nor evil speaking"; or nervous about my challenge to "see that all the members do their duty" (D&C 20:53–55), I am reminded of the sterling example of my old home teaching companion, and I recall the sweet success that came to us and to the families themselves. That season in my young life was in very deed a time that mattered.

We aren't necessarily called to serve in a particular capacity because we have a special talent for that task, nor should the bishop of a ward feel compelled to put in place leaders who have had experience in that realm of Church service. We are not always—maybe I should say that we are seldom—called to serve in a position that is perfectly comfortable to us. The fact of the matter is that it is that discomfort, that required adjustment, that spiritual shaping of ourselves to fit and assume the new assignment, that fosters spiritual growth and true character development. Most calls to serve will require substantial moves outside our comfort zone, whether that be the call to serve as the Primary president, the scoutmaster, the Laurel adviser, the ward mission leader, the Gospel Doctrine teacher, or the nursery leader. It is the stretching that results in the sanctification of the soul.

Strictly speaking, in the Church there is no upward mobility, nor does it even make sense to suggest that a man or woman is moving up the ecclesiastical ladder. Why? Because before you know it, that dynamic stake president has been released and called to teach the eight-year-olds in Primary. Without warning, that spiritually mature Relief Society president has been released after three years of faithful service and called to work in the library.

One of the heartwarming things about the temple is that temple worship is a great leveler. Sitting beside me, dressed in the same white clothing I am wearing, is the president of a college or the CEO of a billion-dollar company or the head football coach at a university or the young man who is soon to be a full-time missionary. In the Church there are no pecking orders: we are all brethren, and successful Church service is often associated with forgetting one's self and focusing intently on the assignment. President Lorenzo Snow spoke of "reading an anecdote . . . of a man who, through his wisdom and patriotism, had gained great renown, but who through envy was assigned to a position which was considered very degrading. On entering upon its duties it was said that he made this significant remark: 'If the office does not honor me I will honor the office.' Much difficulty would be avoided, and our condition and situation would be much more encouraging if we all honored the office in which we are called to act" (*Teachings of Lorenzo Snow*, 99).

Think about what we do when we look at an object through a magnifying glass. The glass causes us to narrow and focus our attention on the object, which we now see with new eyes, as it were. We see things about that spider or that rock or that seashell that we would never have supposed existed; we see details and particulars that come only from an extended period of focus. Using this same analogy, Stephen R. Covey wrote years ago: "All of us are interested in things outside of our stewardship, and we should be, but the most important way to do anything about them is to magnify our own stewardship. This builds trust and confidence and our responsibilities and opportunities to influence increase. . . .

"Take a magnifying glass and notice how it enlarges that which it is placed over and how blurry your peripheral vision is. Now remove the glass. Observe your tendency to look all around the thing you focused on earlier. Where a person focuses on his own responsibility, he becomes relatively unconcerned with other people's stewardships. But when he doesn't magnify his own stewardship and is not a light himself, he looks at the stewardship of everybody else and becomes a judge" (*Spiritual Roots,* 137).

Thus a significant part of magnifying my own life calling entails periodic moments of introspection. "Now let us confess it," President Harold B. Lee observed, "all of us are 'sinners anonymous.' All of us have done things we ought not to have done, or we have neglected things we should have done; and every one of us has need for repentance. So let us not, as President [Wilford] Woodruff said, spend too much time confessing the other fellow's sins. Ours is the responsibility to find our own need for repentance" (*Teachings of Harold B. Lee,* 106–7).

There is a tender experience in the New Testament that illustrates this point. Jesus Christ had spent three years teaching and preparing his chosen apostles, readying them for a time when he would no longer be personally present with them. During his last week in mortality, on the solemn evening before his crucifixion, he met with them for what we have come to know as the Last Supper. "And the disciples did as Jesus had appointed them; and they made ready the

Passover. Now when the even was come, he sat down with the twelve. And as they did eat, he said, Verily I say unto you, that one of you shall betray me" (Matthew 26:19–21).

Let's pause for a moment. Imagine that you are one of the Twelve. You and your eleven apostolic colleagues have walked and talked and listened and eaten and slept and toiled beside the Savior for almost three years. Yours has been a sacred fellowship, a brotherhood like none other. Your devotion to the Master has become solid and secure. Your awe and admiration for him have been transformed into adoration. Your righteous fascination with his way of ministering—his unparalleled love, his tender regard for individuals, his powerful discernment and wisdom, and his transcendent teachings—has morphed into emulation; he has become the pattern for your life, "the prototype or standard of salvation," the embodiment of what it is to be a saved being (*Lectures on Faith*, 75–76, 79). And now the Master announces that one of your number will betray him! How could this be? What would possess one who has been in intimate association with the Son of God to do such a horrendous thing?

Now these twelve men, though noble and loyal and certainly obedient, were in fact men, mortals who lived in a fallen world. A reader of the New Testament would thus expect in this time of terror, this point of panic, that the apostles would hear whispers such as "I know who it is—it's Matthew, the dreadful tax collector, that agent of the Roman empire," or "I'll bet it's Nathaniel, who wondered how any good thing could come out of Nazareth," or "It's pretty clear who the betrayer is. It's got to be Judas Iscariot. He's been acting really strangely in the past few weeks." We would not be surprised to read such reactions. But instead, we read, "And they were exceeding sorrowful, and began every one of them to say unto him, Lord, is it I?" (Matthew 26:22; see also Uchtdorf, *Ensign,* November 2014, 56). What a tribute to these most unusual ministers of the word, these friends of the Bridegroom. How apostolic was their reaction. They looked first within their own hearts.

President Thomas S. Monson asked the men of the priesthood: "What does it mean to magnify a calling? It means to build it up in dignity and importance, to make it honorable and commendable in the eyes of all men, to enlarge and strengthen it, to let the light of heaven shine through it to the view of other men. And how does one magnify a calling? Simply by performing the service that pertains to it. An elder magnifies the ordained calling of an elder, so with . . . each who holds office in the priesthood" (*Ensign,* May 1986, 38–39).

Jacob, son of Lehi, has left us this sobering scriptural treasure: "I, Jacob, and my brother Joseph had been consecrated priests and teachers of this people, by the hand of Nephi. And we did magnify our office unto the Lord, taking upon us the responsibility, *answering the sins of the people upon our own heads if we did not teach them the word of God with all diligence;* wherefore, by laboring with our might their blood might not come upon our garments; otherwise their blood would come upon our garments, and we would not be found spotless at the last day" (Jacob 1:18–19; emphasis added). As President John Taylor taught us: "If you do not magnify your calling, God will hold you responsible for those you might have saved, had you done your duty" (*John Taylor*, 164).

As we contemplate how and in what manner we can better magnify our respective callings, let's consider three individuals in the scriptures from whose lives we can learn a lasting lesson.

The first is a man we have heard about a great deal over the years. He is the man in the parable of the talents who did not improve upon the talents that had been given to him as a stewardship. Two other men are also spoken of in the parable: one who received five talents and one who received two talents. Both these men managed to double what they had been given. They both received the comforting commendation: "Well done, thou good and faithful servant; thou hast been faithful over a few things, I will make thee ruler over many things: enter thou into the joy of thy lord" (Matthew 25:21; see also v. 23).

But what about the other man in the parable, the fellow who was given only one talent and chose to bury it? Why would he do that? Note his defense: "Lord, *I knew that thou art a hard man*, reaping where thou hast not sown, and gathering where thou hast not strawed: and *I was afraid*, and went and hid thy talent in the earth" (Matthew 25:24–25; emphasis added).

Interesting, isn't it? He hid the talent because he, the agent, was frightened of his principal, the one to whom he would be required to render an accounting. His fear of his master motivated him to do nothing.

Given that the one dispensing the talents in the parable

is a type of Christ, how do we apply the parable to our own lives? The unprofitable servant had a serious problem: he didn't really know his lord, and so he was motivated by fear. Perhaps you have seen such a thing in others you know; maybe you have seen it in yourself. She does her duty because she does not want to be punished or banished or disowned by God. He attends to his stewardship because he doesn't want to be required to face the stake president if the job is not done well. I suppose that serving out of fear is better than not carrying out the assigned task at all. But it is not very comforting and not very healthy, either spiritually or emotionally. It certainly isn't very rewarding.

Tragically, doing our duty out of fear arises from a flawed perspective of Deity. Neither the Father nor the Son is hiding just outside the visible world, eager to pounce and catch us in a mistake. Individuals who suppose that do not understand the mercy and goodness of the Lord Jesus Christ or have not felt the lifting, liberating, and soul-settling love of God in their heart as they should. In speaking of our Heavenly Father, C. S. Lewis put it this way: "This Helper who will, in the long run, be satisfied with nothing less than absolute perfection, will also be delighted with the first feeble, stumbling effort you make tomorrow to do the simplest duty" (*Mere Christianity*, 174). Of course. How could it be otherwise?

For our purposes now, let's rewrite the parable. Let us suppose that the man who was given the one talent took it and went to work. He did everything in his power to multiply it, expand it, and build upon it. He labored tirelessly to be a worthy agent and to carry out the wishes of his principal.

But alas, at the end of the season of labor when the master returned, the man still only had one talent. What would the lord of those servants do? What would he say? I firmly believe he would say: "Well done, thou good and faithful servant: thou hast been faithful over a few things, I will make thee ruler over many things: enter thou into the joy of thy Lord" (Matthew 25:21). Why? Because the man would have done the best he possibly could, would have given it his best shot. And that is all God asks of any of us.

Now to the second individual in the scriptures I want to focus on briefly. This man is one with whom even many Latter-day Saints are unfamiliar. In Doctrine and Covenants 117, three men were given specific assignments: William Marks, president of the Kirtland Stake; Newel K. Whitney, bishop in Kirtland; and Oliver Granger, the Prophet's agent, or attorney-in-fact, in Kirtland. The first two men, William Marks and Newel K. Whitney, were counseled to settle their affairs and move to Missouri with the remainder of the Saints. It appears that both of them were striving to acquire some extra cash from the sale of Kirtland properties, and this "littleness of soul" displeased the Lord. "Let them repent of all their sins, and of all their covetous desires, before me, saith the Lord; for what is property unto me?" (D&C 117:11, 4).

The third man addressed by the Savior was Oliver Granger, the Prophet's agent in Kirtland. "Oliver Granger was a very ordinary man," President Boyd K. Packer noted. "He was mostly blind, having 'lost his sight by cold and exposure' (*History of the Church*, 4:408). The First Presidency described him as 'a man of the most strict integrity and moral virtue; and in fine, to be a man of God' (*History of the Church,* 3:350.)

"When the Saints were driven from Kirtland, Ohio, in a scene that would be repeated in Independence, Far West, and in Nauvoo, Oliver was left behind to sell their properties for what little he could. There was not much chance that he could succeed. And, really, he did not succeed!

"But the Lord said, 'Let him contend earnestly for the redemption of the First Presidency of my Church, saith the Lord; and when he falls he shall rise again, for his sacrifice shall be more sacred unto me than his increase, saith the Lord' (D&C 117:13).

"What did Oliver Granger do that his name should be held in sacred remembrance? Nothing much, really. It was not so much what he *did* as what he *was*" (*Ensign,* November 2004, 86; emphasis added).

The words of Doctrine and Covenants 117:13 have fascinated me for years: "And *when he falls he shall rise again, for his sacrifice shall be more sacred unto me than his increase,* saith the Lord" (emphasis added). This passage is one that fills my soul with hope, with optimism, with excitement about the truth that the all-righteous and holy Being we worship will work with us, be patient with us, and offer us an opportunity to get up and dust ourselves off whenever we fall.

President Packer continued in his general conference message: "Some worry endlessly over missions that were missed, or marriages that did not turn out, or babies that did not arrive, or children that seem lost, or dreams unfulfilled, or because age limits what they can do. *I do not think it pleases*

*the Lord when we worry because we think we never do enough or
that what we do is never good enough.*

"Some needlessly carry a heavy burden of guilt which
could be removed through confession and repentance.

"The Lord did not say of Oliver, '*[If]* he falls,' but '*When*
he falls he shall rise again' (D&C 117:3)" (*Ensign,* November
2004, 87; emphasis added).

Character is not a product of a sinless life, not a result
of never making a mistake or an error in judgment, but
rather of never staying down once we have fallen. We show
what we're made of and we show our determination to follow Christ by getting up one more time than we fall. In so
doing, we demonstrate our acceptance of the divine offer to
us to re-group, re-work, re-trust, and re-commit ourselves
to the Christian life and to the accomplishment of our duties. "Time marches on," said President Thomas S. Monson.
"Duty keeps cadence with that march. Duty does not dim
nor diminish. Catastrophic conflicts come and go, but the
war waged for the souls of men continues without abate-
ment" (*Ensign,* May 1986, 37).

Our character will largely be determined by the extent to
which we do on earth what we came here to do. That man
who strives to learn his duty and act in the office in which
he is appointed—that is, magnifies his callings in the priesthood (see D&C 107:99)—is building and refining and sanctifying his character. The work of the priesthood goes forward
on both sides of the veil, and the commission given to those
who bear that priesthood and thus labor for the salvation of
souls will remain in effect until the Messiah returns to earth

and assumes his rightful place as King of kings and Lord of lords. In the meantime, those of us who have been chosen to bear and honor God's holy priesthood are charged to magnify the callings we receive under the direction of those who hold the proper keys. To the extent that we do just that, we will find joy and deep satisfaction in our personal ministries and begin to experience more fully the sanctifying influence of the Spirit in our lives.

POINTS TO PONDER

1. Why would the Lord choose the word magnify to describe what we are charged to do with our callings in the Church? What are some possible meanings of that word?

2. We have been instructed that "inasmuch as ye are agents, ye are on the Lord's errand" (D&C 64:29). What is an agent? How does this relate to my calling as a priesthood holder?

3. What begins to happen when we begin to magnify our callings in the Church? How do you think we change?

4. How did Jesus Christ magnify his calling? How did Joseph Smith magnify his? What do we learn from these great examples of faithfulness?

RECEIVE THE
LORD'S SERVANTS

KARL G. MAESER, A GERMAN IMMIGRANT to the United States, was called by President Brigham Young to serve as the first president of what eventually became Brigham Young University. In speaking of Brother Maeser, President Boyd K. Packer said: "On one occasion he was leading a party of young missionaries across the Alps. As they slowly ascended the steep slope, he looked back and saw a row of sticks thrust into the glacial snow to mark the one safe path across the otherwise treacherous mountains.

"Something about those sticks impressed him, and halting the company of missionaries he gestured toward them and said, 'Brethren, there stands the priesthood. They are just common sticks like the rest of us—some of them may even seem to be a little crooked, but the position they hold makes them what they are. If we step aside from the path they mark, we are lost'" (*That All May be Edified*, 244). Although today we would not refer to the men themselves as the priesthood, Brother Maeser's message is both timely and timeless: safety and security are to be found in following the path laid out by the Lord's servants.

I would like to mention two principal channels of divine power, means by which the Lord extends his goodness and grace and the companionship of his Spirit to the members of the Church of Jesus Christ. One channel is fairly obvious—personal righteousness. That is, to the extent that we as the children of an omniscient and omniloving God strive to abide by his commandments, to align ourselves with his righteous principles and precepts, to keep ourselves free from waywardness and worldliness, our Heavenly Father endows us with light and truth and peace and perspective. "He that keepeth his commandments," the revelations declare, "receiveth truth and light, until he is glorified in truth and knoweth all things" (D&C 93:28). Or, as we are told elsewhere, "That which is of God is light; and he that receiveth light, and continueth in God, receiveth more light; and that light groweth brighter and brighter until the perfect day" (D&C 50:24), meaning, presumably, the time of resurrection.

As members of the Church, when we magnify our callings and fulfill our duties in the Church, we receive the blessings of participation in the Church and the attendant privileges of the priesthood. Then we begin to appreciate what the Lord meant when he explained that in the ordinances of the priesthood "the power of godliness is manifest" (D&C 84:20).

A second channel of divine power and strength, a second means by which our gracious God extends a portion of his power to us, is the quiet outpouring we receive as we are loyal to the Lord's anointed servants. In speaking to his meridian Twelve, the Savior taught, "He that receiveth you receiveth me, and he that receiveth me receiveth him that sent me" (Matthew 10:40).

Isn't that exactly what the Lord explains to us as he sets forth the terms and conditions of the oath and covenant of the Melchizedek Priesthood?

"And also all they who receive this priesthood receive me, saith the Lord; for he that receiveth my servants receiveth me; and he that receiveth me receiveth my Father" (D&C 84:35–37). The Master explained to Thomas B. Marsh and the first apostles called in this final dispensation: "Whosoever receiveth my word receiveth me, and whosoever receiveth me, receiveth those, the First Presidency, whom I have sent" (D&C 112:20).

At the April 1974 general conference of the Church, Elder Bruce R. McConkie offered the following poignant and poetic counsel:

> We be Abraham's children, the Jews said to Jove [Jehovah];
> We shall follow our Father, inherit his trove.
> But from Jesus our Lord, came the stinging rebuke:
> Ye are children of him, whom ye list to obey;
> Were ye Abraham's seed, ye would walk in his path,
> And escape the strong chains of the father of wrath.
>
> We have Moses the seer, and the prophets of old;
> All their words we shall treasure as silver and gold.
> But from Jesus our Lord, came the sobering voice:

If to Moses ye turn, then give heed to his word;

Only then can ye hope for rewards of great worth,

For he spake of my coming and labors on earth.

We have Peter and Paul, in their steps let us trod;

So religionists say, as they worship their God.

But speaks He who is Lord of the living and dead:

In the hands of those prophets, those teachers and seers,

Unto them ye must turn, the Eternal to please.

(*Ensign*, May 1974, 72)

We live in interesting times. During the past five years I have met with a surprising number of Latter-day Saints, young and old, who feel that they want to take an alternate path to salvation than the Church of Jesus Christ; they want to come to God in their way, without some ecclesiastical organization, without some priestly hierarchy. Some suggest that they can draw close to the Almighty in the mountains, while paddling their canoe and absorbing the beauty of nature. Others are fully persuaded that spirituality is completely personal and has little or nothing to do with the Church. Some have chosen to pursue the path of mysticism and to focus on the attainment of higher levels of consciousness.

Don't get me wrong. I love the mountains and delight to be out on a river; few things are more relaxing or therapeutic to me than returning to nature. And I am drawn to deepen my communion with the Infinite. But this state of mind presumes that we can make our way along the strait and narrow path on our own terms, supposedly by simplifying things, by taking the quick and easy route.

The fact of the matter is that we need the Church. A lack of formal organization eventually results in chaos, in every person becoming his own priest and prophet, his own scriptural interpreter. We need the fellowship of the Saints, since true Christianity is always manifest in community, in a body of believers who labor to establish Zion. We need the ordinances and the priesthood authority to administer them (the sacrament of the Lord's Supper, baptism, conferral of the gift of the Holy Ghost, ordinations, endowments, and sealings). We need the teachings and precepts that come from inspired gospel instruction and discussion—we are saved no faster than we get knowledge, the Prophet Joseph told us (see *Joseph Smith,* 266) And we need the leaders of the Church, both general and local, for their oversight and direction and also for the divine power and strength that come through humbly following the counsel of those holding the keys.

It is inevitable in a lay church like ours, which is exactly what the first-century Christian Church was and the restored Church is, that we will come face to face with differences in point of view, oddities and peculiarities, and even serious mistakes. It is hard to imagine that as members of the restored Church we would not have occasion during a lifetime in which decisions were made with which one or another of us disagreed; in which policies or procedures were put in place that rubbed us the wrong way; in which the style of leadership of a new bishop or stake president made us uncomfortable.

That comes with the turf of mortality, doesn't it? Don't human beings regularly see things differently quite often?

Our task as followers of Christ is to love and pray for and uphold our leaders, knowing full well that they have their challenges and are not perfect. We must learn to adapt to differences in administrative styles, knowing that few people on earth will operate in just the same way the previous beloved bishop or stake president did. We must learn to receive the words of our seers and revelators "in all patience and faith" (D&C 21:5), knowing that sometimes we are required to wait for a season before we understand completely why the Brethren counseled as they did. I would ask you a question I have heard my Brigham Young University colleague Shon Hopkin ask: "Do you really want to belong to a church that is created in your image?" Seriously, is it even possible to conceive of a church whose leaders and decisions are in complete harmony with you one hundred percent of the time? That is highly unlikely, if not impossible.

No, our leaders are not perfect. We do not believe in prophetic or apostolic infallibility. And yet, as President David O. McKay taught the Latter-day Saints: "Recognize those who preside over you, and when necessary, seek their advice. . . . Let us, too, recognize the local authority. The bishop may be a humble man. Some of you may think you are superior to him, and you may be, but he is given authority direct from our Father in heaven. You recognize it. Recognition of authority is an important principle" (Conference Report, October 1965, 105).

While we love the scriptures and thank God regularly for

them, we know that we can have confidence and even reverence for holy writ without believing that every word between Genesis 1:1 and Revelation 22:21 is the word-for-word dictation of the Almighty or that the Bible now reads as it has always read. Indeed, our own scriptures attest that plain and precious truths and many covenants of the Lord were taken away or kept back from the Bible before it was compiled (see 1 Nephi 13:20–29; Moses 1:40–41; Articles of Faith 1:8; *Joseph Smith*, 207). But we still cherish the sacred volume, recognize and teach the doctrines of salvation within it, and seek to pattern our lives according to its timeless teachings.

In like manner, we can sustain with all our hearts the prophets and apostles without believing that they are perfect or that everything they say or do is exactly what God wants said and done. Moses made mistakes, but we love and sustain him and accept his writings nonetheless. Peter made mistakes, but we still honor him and study his words. Paul made mistakes, but we admire his boldness and dedication and we treasure his epistles. James pointed out that Elijah "was a man subject to like passions as we are" (James 5:17). The Prophet Joseph declared: "I told them I was but a man, and they must not expect me to be perfect; if they expected perfection from me, I should expect it from them; but if they would bear with my infirmities and the infirmities of the brethren, I would likewise bear with their infirmities" (*Joseph Smith*, 522). "I can fellowship the President of the Church," said Lorenzo Snow, "if he does not know everything I know. . . . I saw the. . . imperfections in [Joseph Smith]. . . . I thanked God that he would put upon a man who had those imperfections the power and authority he placed upon him . . . for I knew that I myself had weakness, and I thought there was a chance for me" (in Maxwell, *Ensign*, November 1984, 10)

As we have been reminded again and again, whom God calls, God qualifies. That is, God calls his prophets. He empowers and strengthens the individual, provides an eternal perspective, loosens his tongue, and enables him to make known divine truth. But being called as an apostle or as president of the Church does not remove the man from mortality or make him perfect. President David O. McKay explained on more than one occasion that "when God makes the prophet He does not unmake the man" (Conference Reports, April 1907, 11–12; October 1912, 121; April 1962, 7).

The Prophet Joseph Smith said: "I was this morning introduced to a man from the east. After hearing my name, he remarked that I was nothing but a man, indicating by this expression, that he had supposed that a person to whom the Lord should see fit to reveal His will, must be something more than a man. He seemed to have forgotten the saying that fell from the lips of St. James, that [Elijah] was a man subject to like passions as we are, yet he had such power with God, that He, in answer to his prayers, shut the heavens that they gave no rain for the space of three years and six months" (*Joseph Smith*, 521).

President Gordon B. Hinckley stated: "I have worked with seven Presidents of this Church. I have recognized that all have been human. But I have never been concerned over this. They may have had some weaknesses. But this has never troubled me. I know that the God of heaven has used mortal men throughout history to accomplish His divine purposes" (*Ensign,* May 1992, 53).

On another occasion President Hinckley pleaded with the Saints that "as we continue our search for truth . . . we look for strength and goodness rather than weakness and foibles in those who did so great a work in their time. We recognize that our forebears were human. They doubtless made mistakes. . . . There was only one perfect man who ever walked the earth. The Lord has used imperfect people in the process of building his perfect society. If some of them occasionally stumbled, or if their characters may have been slightly flawed in one way or another, the wonder is the greater that they accomplished so much" (*Ensign,* April 1986, 5).

"It should be remembered," said Elder D. Todd Christofferson, "that not every statement made by a Church leader, past or present, necessarily constitutes doctrine. It is commonly understood in the Church that a statement made by one leader on a single occasion often represents a personal, though well-considered, opinion, not meant to be official or binding for the whole Church" (*Ensign,* May 2012, 88).

Elder Jeffrey R. Holland encouraged us: "Brothers and sisters, this is a divine work in process, with the manifestations and blessings of it abounding in every direction. . . . So be kind regarding human frailty—your own as well as that of those who serve with you in a Church led by volunteer, mortal men and women. Except in the case of His only perfect Begotten Son, imperfect people are all God has ever had to work with. That must be terribly frustrating to Him, but

He deals with it. So should we. And when you see imperfection, remember that the limitation is not in the divinity of the work" (*Ensign*, May 2013, 93–94).

Finally, President Dieter F. Uchtdorf declared: "Some struggle with unanswered questions about things that have been done or said in the past. We openly acknowledge that in nearly 200 years of Church history—along with an uninterrupted line of inspired, honorable, and divine events—there have been some things said and done that could cause people to question. . . .

"And, to be perfectly frank, there have been times when members or leaders in the Church have simply made mistakes. There may have been things said or done that were not in harmony with our values, principles, or doctrine.

"I suppose the Church would be perfect only if it were run by perfect beings. God is perfect, and His doctrine is pure. But He works through us—His imperfect children—and imperfect people make mistakes" (*Ensign*, November 2013, 22–24).

Prophets are men called of God to serve as covenant spokesmen for his children on earth, and thus we should never take lightly what they say. The early Brethren of this dispensation were the living prophets for their contemporaries, and much of what we believe and practice today rests upon the doctrinal foundation they laid. But the work of the Restoration is in many ways a work in progress; it entails a gradual unfolding of divine truth in a line-upon-line fashion. Some years ago my friend Joseph Fielding McConkie remarked to a group of religious educators: "We have the scholarship of the early brethren to build upon; we have the advantage of additional history; we have inched our way up the mountain of our destiny and now stand in a position to see things with greater clarity than did they. . . .

"We live in finer houses than did our pioneer forefathers, but this does not argue that we are better or that our rewards will be greater. In like manner our understanding of gospel principles should be better housed, and we should constantly be seeking to make it so. There is no honor in our reading by oil lamps when we have been granted better light" ("Gathering of Israel," 3, 5).

Ultimately the Lord will hold us responsible for heeding the teachings and direction and focus provided by the living oracles of our own day, both in terms of their commentary upon canonized scripture, as well as the living scripture delivered through them by the power of the Holy Ghost (see D&C 68:3–4). Until the day comes when "he reigns whose right it is to reign, and subdues all enemies under his feet" (D&C 58:22), the Saints of the Most High have been counseled and commissioned to receive the prophetic word "in all patience and faith" (D&C 21:5).

Let me share an experience that affirms that very often we do not see things as they really are when it comes to those called to lead us. Shauna and I had been married only a little over a year when we moved into a ward in which I found myself beginning to harbor feelings I had never felt before. I didn't like our bishop! He was a good man, I was sure, one who was capable enough, one who had much Church experience. But he seemed so unfriendly, so cold, so unapproachable. We were in the ward for several weeks before I said something to Shauna about it. She responded that she didn't think he was cold; he seemed like a nice man to her. I concluded that she simply wasn't paying attention. The feelings got worse, and I found myself mentioning it a couple of times to my wife.

One Sunday afternoon, just before she was to leave for a leadership meeting, she said to me: "Bob, you've got a problem. You had better deal with it, or you're going to be in trouble." My first reaction was that she was overstating the case, but I knew deep down that she was right on target with her assessment. I knew I had to do something.

Providentially, Shauna was at her meetings for a few hours, leaving me all alone with my thoughts and my problem. I prayed with great intensity. I confessed my sin to him who knows the thoughts and intents of the human heart. I acknowledged that I could not do this on my own. I realized that it was a matter not just of refraining from speaking evil of the Lord's anointed but of rooting out my attitude.

Thankfully, in time things began to change. I remember sitting in sacrament meeting and looking up to the stand. I stared at our bishop, and a whole new set of feelings came into my heart. I felt compassion for that good man. I felt gratitude for an extremely busy man, one who because of his job had little free time but who had accepted a call to serve in a demanding position. I felt that the Lord loved him. And then, in a most unexpected manner, I was filled with love for him.

Let me now tell you the rest of the story. This much

would have been an experience with valuable lessons if the story had ended there. But it did not. Within a short time—if my memory is right, it was within a couple of weeks—I received a phone call one evening. The stake executive secretary asked if I would be willing to meet with the stake president the next afternoon up on campus. I agreed. The next day I entered the stake president's office filled with fear and trembling. I had no idea what this was about. I sat down, and he began with a very thorough worthiness interview. That got my attention. He then inquired, "Brother Millet, are you willing to accept a call in this Church, one that will require a great deal of time and energy?" I held my breath but answered that I was. He then said: "On Sunday we will be making a change in your ward bishopric. The second counselor to the bishop is being released, and Bishop Sherwood has asked that you serve in that capacity. Are you willing to accept this assignment?"

I was absolutely dumbfounded. Breathless. Unable to utter a word. The stake president sensed my discomfort and added: "Comes as a surprise, doesn't it?"

I thought to myself: "You have no idea!"

He then asked a question that startled and stunned me: "Now, Brother Millet, can you offer your love, as well as your full loyalty and support, to Bishop Sherwood?"

I said that I would do so.

My experience in that bishopric was life changing. I learned so much. And I learned it from a fine teacher, Bishop Sherwood, a man who, though shy, proved to be extremely warm and friendly and loving. I have thought a hundred times since then: What would my situation have been if I had not dealt with my problem? What if I had not made the effort to go to the Lord, open myself to change, and allow his supernal power to make me into a new man? What lessons would I have missed, what opportunities to minister to the Saints and serve them, what spiritual growth would have been denied me, if I had allowed myself to fester in my shortsighted, judgmental feelings? President Harold B. Lee taught us many years ago that a person is "not truly converted until he sees the power of God resting upon the leaders of this Church and it goes down into his heart like fire" (*Stand Ye in Holy Places*, 62).

This conversion does not come cheap; it is a precious gift of the Spirit that must be sought and pleaded for. God grants this gift.

Again, as holders of the priesthood of Almighty God, you and I are charged to receive the Lord's servants. That means we are to honor them, respect them, listen carefully to what they teach us, and then hearken to—that is, hear and obey—their counsel. The only way we can escape or deflect the fiery darts of the adversary, make it through mortality safely, and find ourselves on the Lord's side of the line, is to come to see things as the Brethren see them.

We sustain fifteen men as prophets, seers, and revelators. Seers are men who have received the divine endowment that enables them to "see things which [are] not visible to the natural eye" (Moses 6:36). These living oracles have it given to them to see the distant scene, far down the road of life, and in some cases to see things that are just around the corner. To "follow the Brethren" is to feel what they feel about things, especially tough issues in our society—threats to our religious liberty, matters of sexual morality, and the preservation and perpetuation of traditional marriage and family, to name only a few. We must fight manfully against falling into what President Packer called the "tolerance trap" (*Ensign,* May 2013, 8)—the tendency to allow tolerance of another's point of view or lifestyle to color and taint our view of what is right and wrong.

We are richly blessed to be led by men with seeric vision, prophets and apostles who for our sakes have sought to sanctify themselves (see John 17:19) so that they may deliver the mind and will of God to God's people. For our part, we can show our appreciation for this level of consecration by being a people who are easy to be entreated, a society of Saints who prove by their devotion and loyalty that they are intelligently obedient.

To enjoy the spiritual power that comes only to those who are loyal to the Lord's anointed, we must ensure that we see what the leaders of the Church see and feel what the leaders of the Church feel. As President Lee said: "One is converted when he sees with his eyes what he ought to see; when he hears with his ears what he ought to hear; and when he understands with his heart what he ought to understand. And what he ought to see, hear, and understand is truth—eternal truth—and then practice it. That is conversion" (*Stand Ye in Holy Places,* 92).

Let us remind ourselves of what the Lord has promised to those who give heed to the words and commandments of

God that come to us through our prophets: "For by doing these things the gates of hell shall not prevail against you; yea, and the Lord God will disperse the powers of darkness from before you" (D&C 21:6). That is, the power and dominion of the devil will not overcome us. Like Jesus Christ, our light will shine in darkness, and the darkness will not be able to comprehend it, meaning, darkness will not be able to take in, overpower, or gain control over our souls (see John 1:5; D&C 88:49). Finally, our Lord will "cause the heavens to shake for [our] good, and his name's glory" (D&C 21:6). Indeed, God will move heaven and earth for those who demonstrate their loyalty to him by being loyal to his chosen servants. We could not ask for more!

POINTS TO PONDER

1. Why are prophets, seers, and revelators called? What functions do they serve on the earth?

2. What is your relationship to the prophets and apostles today? How are they linked to your salvation?

3. What would you say to a person in the Church who stated that he or she was very devoted to the Savior but did not feel any need to honor the prophets and apostles?

4. Why is it that to receive the Lord's servants is to receive the Lord himself?

BEWARE CONCERNING OURSELVES

THOSE OF US WHO HAVE RECEIVED the Melchizedek Priesthood are called to live in a state of spiritual vigilance. We are to be on the lookout, on our toes, always watching, ever attentive to detours, distractions, and destructive behaviors and attitudes. In the words of the Savior, we are to "take heed to yourselves" (Mark 13:9). This passage strikes me as a sobering warning to us to see that we do not get in the way of the Lord's work, a charge that we not be the problem. Let's consider some specific areas of concern.

First of all, let us ask ourselves where the affections of our soul are directed. The Savior in his marvelous Sermon on the Mount sounded this warning:

"Lay not up for yourselves treasures upon earth, where moth and rust doth corrupt, and where thieves break through and steal: but lay up for yourselves treasures in heaven, where neither moth nor rust doth corrupt, and where thieves do not break through nor steal: for *where your treasure is, there will your heart be also*" (Matthew 6:19–22; emphasis added).

That is a perceptive lesson: my heart will be where my treasures are. Or, to put it another way, the spiritual quality of my soul will be determined by those things on which I focus most of my time, attention, and energy. Why? Because "as a man thinketh in his heart, so is he" (Proverbs 23:7). We learn from the scriptures that we cannot serve both God and mammon (meaning money or worldliness; see Matthew 6:24) and, further, that "a double-minded man is unstable in all his ways" (James 1:8).

Hugh Nibley addressed himself to the deceitfulness of riches and man's futile efforts to find happiness and fulfillment in fleeting and ephemeral material possessions: "Why should we labor this unpleasant point? Because the Book of Mormon labors it, for our specific benefit. Wealth is a jealous master who will not be served half-heartedly and will suffer no rival—not even God. . . . In return for unquestioning obedience wealth promises security, power, position, and honors, in fact anything in this world. . . . Along with this, of course, everyone dresses in the height of fashion, the main point being always that the proper clothes are expensive— the expression 'costly apparel' occurs 14 times in the Book of Mormon. *The more important wealth is, the less important it is how one gets it*" (*Since Cumorah,* 393–94; emphasis added).

Brother Nibley's last sentence above is particularly worrisome to me. A friend of mine, a devoted Christian not of our faith, said to me recently, "I have great respect for Mormons, particularly the way they take care of their own and the manner in which they focus so much on the importance of family. But I will never do business with another Latter-day Saint."

Startled by his comment, I asked him to say more. He related that on several occasions during the preceding few years he had been metaphorically taken to the cleaners by devoted, tithe-paying, temple-recommend-holding Saints.

"I just don't get it," he said. "I know these are good people who go to church, attend their temple, and send their children on missions, but when it comes to business dealings, they seem to have no conscience." He told me that he had quite recently confronted a man who was serving in a stake presidency, a man who had just cheated him out of hundreds of thousands of dollars. When he asked the man how he could live with himself when he did such things, the Latter-day Saint priesthood holder smiled and remarked, "Well, I'm just a shrewd businessman."

No, he is a thief, a dishonest member of the Lord's Church who is not living up to his covenants. Somehow he seems to have compartmentalized his life such that he has created a huge chasm between his personal life and standards and his employment and actions permissible there. If that were the only situation of this kind with which I was familiar, I wouldn't even mention it. But sadly, I have encountered it many times. Another scenario I know quite well, since the person who was cheated is a very dear friend. He had worked for almost a year on a job (he is an extremely skilled workman), and his company submitted the bill for his services, a little more than one million dollars. Weeks and months passed as my friend continued to contact the other party, unsuccessfully, in an effort to collect what was owed to him.

Finally, a man, a Latter-day Saint priesthood holder, who represented the other party, approached my friend, held out a check for $200,000, and said, "Take it or leave it." He then said that if my friend was not satisfied with the amount of the check, he could take the other party to court. My friend, who was a recent convert, shook his head and said, "That is tough on a person's faith."

A chilling phrase used in the Pearl of Great Price speaks volumes. Of some of Adam and Eve's children, including Cain and his wife and family, the scriptural account says: "They loved Satan more than God" (Moses 5:13, 18, 28). It isn't that they didn't love God; they just loved Satan and the allurements of this telestial world more.

A second matter we should be concerned with relates to letters written from Liberty Jail, those powerful and revelatory instructions given by the Prophet Joseph while he was a prisoner there (see D&C 121–23). Some of my favorite passages of scripture are found in those sections of the Doctrine and Covenants. Section 121 is especially meaningful to me. There we learn that "there are many called, but few are chosen." Why? "Because their hearts are set so much upon the things of this world, and aspire to the honors of men, that they do not learn this one lesson—that the rights of the priesthood are inseparably connected with the powers of heaven, and that the powers of heaven cannot be controlled nor handled only upon the principles of righteousness" (D&C 121:34–36).

Then the Prophet speaks of how "it is the nature and disposition of almost all men, as soon as they get a little authority, as they suppose, they will immediately begin to exercise unrighteous dominion" (D&C 121:39). He then goes on to explain beautifully the kinds of qualities and attributes that characterize righteous leadership (see D&C 121:41–46).

President John Taylor stated the same principle a little differently. "There is a priesthood in the heavens," he explained, "and we have the same priesthood on the earth, but there should be *a closer communion between the priesthood on the earth and the priesthood in the heavens*; it is desirable that we should be brought into closer proximity; we want to be advancing as Enoch advanced" (*Gospel Kingdom,* 129–30; emphasis added).

Unrighteous dominion. What is it, and how do we avoid it? Every person who is called to a leadership position wants to be successful, wants to fulfill his assignment well, wants to get the job done. But when does he begin to exercise unrighteous dominion? A man exercises unrighteous dominion in his home when he makes all the decisions for the family, when he fails to involve his wife and the children in family affairs, when he rules the home with an iron hand, when he bullies or pressures family members, when his approach to motivation borders on abuse. A leader exercises unrighteous dominion in a ward or branch or stake when he seeks to get the job done at any cost, no matter whose feelings are hurt in the process; when he refuses to delegate properly and assumes all of the burden of responsibility himself; when he does not allow those within the ward leadership to do their jobs and make the appropriate decisions for their respective organizations; when his effort to promote missionary work or activation or the accomplishment of any task comes close to badgering or browbeating the members. Moral agency is a precious, God-given gift, the one gift over which the war in heaven was fought. God will not violate our agency, and a man who does so, does so on his own and without the authority or power of the priesthood. Indeed, of such a man the revelation declares, "Amen to the priesthood or the authority of that man" (D&C 121:37).

Relative to the kind of union and partnership that ought to exist between a priesthood man and his wife, President Spencer W. Kimball taught: "When we speak of marriage as a partnership, let us speak of marriage as a *full* partnership. We do not want our LDS women to be silent partners or limited partners in that eternal assignment! Please be a *contributing* and *full* partner" (*Ensign,* November 1978, 106; emphasis added).

President Howard W. Hunter, in speaking to the men of the Church, was similarly direct: "Presiding in righteousness necessitates a shared responsibility between husband and wife; together you act with knowledge and participation in all family matters. For a man to operate independently of or without regard to the feelings and counsel of his wife in governing the family is to exercise unrighteous dominion" (*Ensign,* November 1994, 51).

We avoid unrighteous dominion by treating every person

as a son or daughter of our Eternal Father; by caring more for our brothers and sisters in the household of faith than we do about success, attention, or popularity; by realizing that the work and glory of God are people (see Moses 1:39); by understanding that this earth was created and the great plan of happiness was put into effect because of people; by seeing to it that people and their feelings are always honored. Of course, effective Church leaders follow the *Handbook* and directives set in place by apostles and prophets, and they are also sensitive to those moments when a slight exception might need to be made. The Lord's list of qualities that ensure that God's precious children are properly honored are the same virtues and attributes the apostle Paul described as the "fruit of the Spirit," those Christlike qualities that flow from the heart of a person who has been changed by Christ (Galatians 5:22; see also v. 23).

A third matter we need to guard against is becoming obsessed with the wickedness of the world. Now this is tough, to be sure. On the one hand, priesthood holders simply must know what's happening in our world, including what the traumas, tragedies, and atrocities all about us are. We cannot bury our head in the sand or pretend that all is well in Zion (see 2 Nephi 28:21). We cannot afford to turn a blind eye to the spread of pornography, the specter of abuse in all its ugly forms, the erosion of time-honored values and individual liberties in society, or the secularization of our world. These things are scary, and they certainly deserve our attention. But what we must not allow ourselves to do is to fixate on evil, to become so consumed with the widening of wickedness and the spread of sin that we allow our conversation, our attitudes, and our perspective on life to become cynical or jaded. We guard against and fight wickedness, but we do not obsess over it.

Jehovah, speaking through Isaiah, asked: "Who among us shall dwell with the devouring fire? Who among us shall dwell with everlasting burnings?" He answered: "He that walketh righteously, and speaketh uprightly; he that despiseth the gain of oppressions, that shaketh his hands from holding bribes, that stoppeth his ears from hearing of blood, and shutteth his eyes from seeing evil; he shall dwell on high" (Isaiah 33:14–16).

A second passage of scripture that has special appeal to me in this connection is from the apostle Paul: "Whatsoever things are true, whatsoever things are honest, whatsoever things are just, whatsoever things are pure, whatsoever things are lovely, whatsoever things are of good report; if there be any virtue, and if there be any praise, *think on these things*" (Philippians 4:8; ; emphasis added; see also Articles of Faith 1:13).

Truly, what we think about will determine what we do and who we become.

And so it is with how we choose to face our trials and our dilemmas. An interesting commandment in scripture is this one: "Thou shalt thank the Lord thy God in all things" (D&C 59:7). Does God need our thanks? Is he somehow bettered when his children thank him? I think not. God is an independent being, and although he loves us perfectly and desires us to be faithful and obedient, his Godhood does not depend on our doing so. Rather, our expressions of thanks and gratitude are for our good. Such declarations draw our attention away from ourselves and our own accomplishments and direct our thoughts to him who is the "Father of lights" (D&C 67:9) and the giver of all good gifts. Only through forgetting self and yielding our hearts to him can we have joy here and eternal reward and glory hereafter. Thus, "in nothing doth man offend God, or against none is his wrath kindled, save those who confess not his hand in all things, and obey not his commandments" (D&C 59:21). And, as President Dieter F. Uchtdorf stated, "I don't believe the Lord expects us to be less thankful in times of trial than in times of abundance and ease. In fact, most of the scriptural references do not speak of gratitude for things but rather suggest an overall spirit or attitude of gratitude." Thus we ought to "see gratitude as a disposition, a way of life that stands independent of our current situation" (*Ensign,* May 2014, 70, 75). That is, "he that receiveth of God, let him account it of God" (D&C 50:34).

I have noticed a tendency in our day that is deeply troubling. In an effort not to appear hyperrighteous, holier-than-thou, or stuffy, and because so often today religious people are marginalized or ignored, some Latter-day Saints have sought to give the impression that yes, they're LDS but not like some of those boring types. They want to be considered (often by younger people) as cool, with it, rad, bad, or whatever the term is these days.

A hypocrite is not one who holds tightly to high standards and ideals but falls short; if that were the case, all of us would be hypocrites, for we are all less than we ought to be and are ever in need of pardoning mercy. No, hypocrisy is just what its Greek name implies: wearing a mask, acting a part, putting on a show, faking it, saying in public how good one is but with evil intent, living in private well below the standards of one's faith.

There is another kind of hypocrisy, less obvious but just as serious. Elder Neal A. Maxwell spoke of it as a "second form of hypocrisy, the situation in which we let ourselves appear worse than we are. This form of hypocrisy is just as insidious (and may be more widespread) than the other form of hypocrisy—the situation in which we let ourselves appear better than we are. The second form . . . is apt to be a heightened challenge because of the growing uniqueness and size of the Church; it will be increasingly tempting for members of the Church to play down their convictions and commitment—to appear less committed than they really are" (*More Excellent Way*, 62–63).

We remember that Paul declared in one of his epistles: "I am not ashamed of the gospel of Christ: for it is the power of God unto salvation" (Romans 1:16). To his beloved helper Timothy, Paul also said: "God hath not given us the spirit of fear; but of power, and of love, and of a sound mind. Be not thou therefore ashamed of the testimony of our Lord" (2 Timothy 1:7–8).

To beware concerning ourselves is to look out for those spiritual stumbling blocks that slow us down, cause us to take detours, or lead us off the narrow way and into forbidden paths. It is to be personally reflective, to be introspective, to look inward on a regular basis. Joseph Smith taught: "If you wish to go where God is, you must be like God, or possess the principles which God possesses, for if we are not drawing towards God in principle, we are going from Him and drawing towards the devil. . . .

"Search your hearts, and see if you are like God. I have searched mine, and feel to repent of all my sins. . . . As far as we degenerate from God, we descend to the devil and lose knowledge, and without knowledge we cannot be saved, and while our hearts are filled with evil, and we are studying evil, there is no room in our hearts for good, or studying good." Now consider these marvelous words, also from the Choice Seer: "Is not God good? Then you be good; *if He is faithful, then you be faithful.* Add to your faith virtue, to virtue knowledge, and seek for every good thing" (*Joseph Smith,* 72, 265–66; emphasis added).

When the rich young man asked Jesus what he must do to inherit eternal life, he was told to keep the commandments. "The young man saith unto him, all these have I kept from my youth up: what lack I yet?" And of course the Savior looked into the core of the young man's soul, discerned quickly his spiritual challenge, and addressed it directly: "If thou wilt be perfect, go and sell that thou hast, and give to the poor, and thou shalt have treasure in heaven: and come and follow me." And of course the rich young man was not able to do so, for he had come to trust in his possessions (Matthew 19:16–22; see also JST Mark 10:26; JST Luke 18:27).

"Notice what has happened," observes N. T. Wright. "The young man has come wanting fulfillment. He wants his life to be complete—complete in the present, so it can be complete in the future. He knows he is still 'lacking' something, and he is looking for a goal, a completion. Jesus suggests that he needs turning inside out. His life is to become part of a larger, outward-looking purpose: he is to put God's kingdom first, and put his neighbor (especially his poor neighbor) before his own fulfillment and prospects. Here is the real challenge: not just to add one or two more commandments, to set the moral bar a little higher, but to *become a different sort of person altogether.* Jesus is challenging the young man to a transformation of character" (*After You Believe,* 15–16; emphasis added).

How ready are you to ask the question, "Lord, what lack I yet?" That is, "Lord, what areas in my life would you like me to repent of, jettison, clean up, work on, develop, perfect?"

Are you willing to do such a thing? I have dared to undertake such a spiritual scrutiny a few times in my life, and it has been extremely humbling and staggeringly informative. I have come to believe that there are certain kinds of prayers that our Heavenly Father is just delighted to answer. When we plead with him to help us become a better father and a more loving husband, he goes to work right away. I believe when we ask him to assist us to become more loving and welcoming to those who are less active, those who are estranged for some reason, even those who are outside our faith, our God, who loves every one of his children perfectly, is eager to respond. And I believe when we are courageous enough to get down on our knees and ask "What lack I yet?"

impressions and ideas and feelings will flood into our minds and hearts without much delay or even much effort on our part.

Our holy God yearns for his children to be at their best, to become "a chosen generation, a royal priesthood, an holy nation, a peculiar people" who "shew forth the praises of him who hath called [us] out of darkness into his marvelous light" (1 Peter 2:9). And so any effort on our part to come to know better where we need to improve and what we need to repent of will be rewarded by the Holy Spirit's guidance and direction. Isn't this what the Lord had in mind when he spoke through Moroni? "And if men come unto me I will show unto them their weakness. I give unto men weakness that they may be humble; and my grace is sufficient for all men that humble themselves before me; for if they humble themselves before me, and have faith in me, then will I make weak things become strong unto them" (Ether 12:27; compare 2 Corinthians 12:7–10).

Our Father in Heaven will surely make known unto us our weakness—our mortality, our fallen nature, our absolute inability to make spiritual progress without the cleansing and transforming powers of the atonement of Jesus Christ. That is, God will reveal to us how dependent we are upon him. He will also make known to us our specific weaknesses, those personality quirks, flaws of character, defects in disposition, areas in interpersonal relationships where we are less than noble, and of course our sins and misdeeds. We must know those things in order to properly repent, be cleansed and renewed, and become a new creation of the Holy Ghost. Our

Father has no desire to keep our sins and our imperfections secret; he is more than willing to give us deeper insights into who we are and where we need to experience lasting change. C. S. Lewis pointed out that "mere improvement is not redemption, although redemption always improves people even here and now and will, in the end, improve them to a degree we cannot yet imagine. God became man to turn creatures into sons: not simply to produce better men of the old kind but to produce a new kind of man" (*Mere Christianity*, 183).

We would call such a being a man of Christ, a priesthood man.

POINTS TO PONDER

1. Why would Satan be especially eager to tempt and lead astray a man who holds the priesthood?

2. Search your heart. Are there things in your life that simply do not befit a chosen servant of God?

3. Why would Joseph Smith state that "it is the nature and disposition of almost all men, as soon as they get a little authority, as they suppose, they will immediately begin to exercise unrighteous dominion"? (D&C 121:39).

4. What can you do to ensure that your life is on course, that the way you live allows you to enjoy power in the priesthood?

LIVE BY EVERY WORD OF GOD

THE PATH TO ETERNAL LIFE in the highest degree of the celestial kingdom is a path of growth, expansion, and spiritual development. At the same time, the path requires significant narrowing and shrinking. Indeed, the extent to which I learn to narrow will determine just how much I will expand. Is that paradox sufficiently clear? Let me explain what I mean.

Each person on earth who receives the gospel of Jesus Christ comes into the Lord's kingdom in what might be called the broad way. The Savior delivered a parable in which he said, "The kingdom of heaven is like unto a net, that was cast into the sea, and gathered of every kind" (Matthew 13:47). The gospel net gathers of every kind—people from every walk of life make their way into the Church of Jesus Christ: poor and wealthy, highly educated and ignorant, deeply religious and skeptical, those seasoned in deep sin and those whose lives have reflected only goodness and nobility. Every type imaginable. This is what I mean when I speak of the broad way—the disciples of the Master are as different as night and day. Some men come into the Church with much baggage and a great deal of cleansing and sanctification yet ahead of them. Others bring to the table of the Lord a life that has been devoted to virtue and discipline and Christian service. Truly, all are welcomed into the kingdom and are invited to come as they are.

But the Savior's parable does not end there. When the gospel net "was full, they drew to shore, and sat down, and gathered the good into vessels, but cast the bad away. So shall it be at the end of the world. And the world is the children of the wicked. The angels shall come forth, and sever the wicked from among the just, and shall cast them out into the world to be burned. There shall be wailing and gnashing of teeth" (JST Matthew 13:48–51).

That sounds a little less welcoming. It is the difference between the day of one's baptism and the Day of Judgment, the difference between what the Lord expects of the initiate, the starter Saint, and what he requires of the seasoned Saint. In other words, one may come into the faith with his or her own proclivities, predispositions, and hang-ups, but the Holy One of Israel expects the sheep of his fold over time to put off the trappings of the natural man or woman and put on Christ, that is, be adorned in the robes of righteousness. Real religion is a process of spiritual refinement, of keeping oneself "unspotted from the vices of the world" (JST James 1:27).

Such a mighty change will come about only through the power of the blood of the Lamb. The repentance and forsaking of sin that must precede such a mighty change entails a great deal of narrowing. That is what Jesus meant when he taught that the gospel path is narrow (see Matthew 7:13–14; D&C 132:22–25). It's a close walk, a tight squeeze, almost requiring us to turn sideways and inch our way through, much like what we experience as we pass through a turnstile. One person at a time can go through, only one. And though membership in the Church of Jesus Christ is lifting and liberating, it also entails a narrowing, a chipping away of the barnacles of sin, a jettisoning of the rudiments of this wicked world, a relinquishing of crudeness, rudeness, and insensitivity.

To put this another way, as I make my way down the narrow gospel path, there are fewer and fewer things I can do and still get away with; my more sensitive conscience and my educated desires will no longer allow me to trifle with truth or to flirt with ungodliness. Elder Orson Pratt described this spiritual refinement as coming to love the things we before hated and hate the things we before loved (*Holy Spirit,* 56–57).

While all of this is quite interesting, what does it have to do with the oath and covenant of the Melchizedek Priesthood? Simply this: the revelation that sets forth the terms and conditions of that covenant includes this proviso: "For you shall live by every word that proceedeth forth from the mouth of God" (D&C 84:44).

We are to live by every word that comes from the Lord. Every word. Not every other word, but *every* word. "At times," Elder Robert D. Hales explained, "members may participate in 'selective obedience,' claiming to love God and honor God while picking and choosing which of His commandments and teachings—and the teachings and counsel of His prophets—they will fully follow.

"Some obey selectively because they cannot perceive all the reasons for a commandment, just as children do not always understand the reasons for their parents' counsel and rules. But we always know the reason we follow the prophets, for this is the Church of Jesus Christ, and it is the Savior who directs His prophets in all dispensations" (*Ensign*, May 2014, 36).

By striving to live by every word of God we open ourselves to new insights, new feelings, new and added pleasures, new perspectives on life here and hereafter. Consider for a moment the rather fascinating manner in which Joshua and the children of Israel were instructed to conquer the city of Jericho by marching around the city so many times, blowing the trumpets at a certain time, etc. (see Joshua 6). It would certainly have been easier for Jehovah to sweep the land of Jericho with fire and destroy all the inhabitants and then have the Israelites move into their new digs. But God didn't do it that way. Rather, he announced a plan that required the descendants of Abraham to give perfect heed to his word, to follow his instructions with exactness—to do things just as their Lord instructed them, down to the minutest detail. That is just what happened with Gideon and his army of three hundred when they defeated the Midianites (see Judges 7), and very similar to how Helaman's stripling warriors met and defeated their Lamanite enemy. Of the sons of Helaman, the record states that "those two thousand and sixty were firm and undaunted. Yea, and *they did obey and observe to perform every word of command with exactness*; yea, and even according to their faith it was done unto them" (Alma 57:20–21; emphasis added). These faithful young men were "true at all times in whatsoever thing they were entrusted. Yea, they were men of truth and soberness, for they had been taught *to keep the commandments of God and to walk uprightly* before him" (Alma 53:20–21; emphasis added).

As holders of the priesthood of the Almighty, we live by every word of God when we devote ourselves to the whole gospel, giving attention to every facet of the faith. A man who is otherwise active in the Church, attending his meetings and taking part, but who refuses to lead his family in a weekly home evening or daily family prayer is not living by every word of God. A man who attends the temple regularly, perhaps even serves as an ordinance worker, but who is rather hit and miss in his assignment as a home teacher, is not living by every word of God. A man who is everybody's friend at Church and is the life of the party at activities but treats his wife and children with disrespect and operates as a tyrant within the walls of his own home is not living by every word of God. The God of Abraham, Isaac, and Jacob spoke through Moses the Lawgiver and said: "Cursed be he that confirmeth not all the words of this law to do them" (Deuteronomy 27:26; compare Galatians 3:10). James the brother of the Lord put it this way: "For whosoever shall keep the whole law, and yet offend [stumble, err] in one point, he is guilty of all" (James 2:10). Or as the Prophet Joseph Smith stated: "The question is frequently asked, 'Can we not be saved without going through with all those ordinances, etc.?' I would answer, No, not the fullness of salvation. Jesus said, 'There are many mansions in my Father's house, and I will go and prepare a place for you.' House here named should have been translated kingdom; and any person who is exalted to the highest mansion has to abide a celestial law, and the whole law too" (*Joseph Smith*, 418).

This counsel is not intended to either overwhelm or depress us; God does not want his covenant sons to languish in guilt because of everything we simply cannot get to. Rather, it is the Lord's way of inviting and encouraging us to enjoy the sweet and satisfying fruits of engaging the whole gospel, of living by every word of God. Let me give an example. As a bishop, I remember very well sitting in my office across the desk from a young woman in her early twenties who had come in to visit with me. After about ten minutes of friendly conversation, we continued our discussion that had been going on for a couple of months. In the previous visits she had expressed her desire to get her life in order and to clear up many of the sinful matters in her past that had managed to creep in during her years of inactivity in the Church. I had given her some assignments (reading, praying for forgiveness, fasting, attending church meetings, giving service), and she wanted to report on how she was doing.

I followed up on a number of matters, particularly the sexual immorality that she had allowed to creep into her life. She indicated that she had broken off the relationship with the young man with whom she had been involved and was trying to bring more and more light into her life by monitoring where she spent her time and with whom. I commended her warmly for her progress and then inquired about her Word of Wisdom problems. My question seemed to startle her, and she responded with these words, as I recall: "Wait a minute, bishop. You can't expect me to repent of sexual sin and of smoking and drinking at the same time! Let me solve one problem at a time. I'm repenting of one thing now, and when that is forgiven and out of the way, I'll move to the next problem and deal with it. Is that okay?"

I wondered for a moment how I might respond in the kindest and most respectful way and yet be able to take advantage of this teaching moment. I explained to my young friend that genuine repentance is our Father in Heaven's gift to us and is available because of the sufferings and death of his Beloved Son, the atoning sufferings that began in the Garden of Gethsemane and were completed on the cross of Calvary. I observed that true repentance is always preceded by faith in the Lord Jesus Christ—in a total trust in him, a complete confidence in his power to forgive us and renovate our souls, a ready reliance upon his merits, mercy, and grace—and that saving repentance requires a whole-souled effort on our part to rid ourselves of all sin, all deviation from the path of righteousness, all offense against God and his commandments. I explained to her that what we were doing was not just cleaning one room of the house. We were engaged in cleaning the whole house, every room, every nook and cranny, so that our house becomes a proper abode for Spirit of the Living God. And so it is with you and me and with our quest to be fully active, fully involved, and fully committed to the whole gospel of Jesus Christ. Dedicated discipleship is a whole-souled endeavor.

One sign of spiritual growth is steadiness, a capacity to navigate the strait and narrow path in a stable and consistent manner, to work with zeal but patient maturity, to stay in the mainstream of the Church. God does not expect us to work ourselves into spiritual, emotional, or physical exhaustion, nor does he desire that the members of the Church be truer than true. There is little virtue in excess, even in gospel excess. In fact, when members of the Church go beyond the established mark, they open themselves to deception and ultimately to destruction. Imbalance leads to instability. If Satan cannot entice us toward sins of commission, it just may be that he will cause our strength—our zeal for goodness and righteousness—to become our weakness. He will encourage excess, for surely any virtue, when taken to the extreme, becomes a vice.

Persons who determine upon a course that will take them beyond the expected, above the required, inevitably begin to expect the same of others. That expectation becomes a principle to which others are proselyted. The overzealous tend to judge others by their own standard. I have known persons who are so completely committed to family history and temple work, for example, that they badger and criticize others who are not in a position to do as much as they are. Obviously, such work is a vital part of our ministry as Latter-day Saints; we neglect it at the peril of our eternal salvation. I also know, as Elder Dallin H. Oaks pointed out, that there is a time and a season for all things, that individuals' specific contributions to the kingdom are and must be private consecrations between the persons and God. This is why the leaders of the Church have discouraged establishing quotas and goals for temple work. "Our efforts to promote temple and family history work," Elder Oaks noted, "should be such as to accomplish the work of the Lord, not to impose guilt on his children. Members of this Church have many individual circumstances—age, health, education, place of residence, family responsibilities, financial circumstances, accessibility to sources for individual or library research, and many others. If we encourage members in this work without taking these individual circumstances into account, we may do more to impose guilt than to further the work. . . . There are many different things our members can do to help in the redeeming of the dead, in temple and family history work. Some involve callings. All are expressions of devotion and discipleship. All present opportunities for sacrifice and service" (*Ensign,* June 1989, 6–7).

What we are being warned against here is a phenomenon known as gospel hobbies, the tendency to take a good thing and run it into the ground. We are speaking of the evils of excess, even in noble and worthwhile causes. Gospel hobbies lead to imbalance. To instability. To distraction. To misperception. They are dangerous and should be avoided as we would any other sin. This brother reads scripture six hours a day, wonders why the other members of his quorum do not follow his example, and, frankly, in the process neglects his wife and children and occasionally his Church callings. That sister fasts three times a week for greater spirituality and repeatedly suggests to the sisters in her ward that they would do well to follow her lead. One family refuses to eat chocolate, white bread, and meat of any kind and wonders why the great majority of the Latter-day Saints do not take the Word of Wisdom seriously.

When we are distracted by gospel hobbies, we are not living by every word of God. President Joseph F. Smith said: "We frequently look about us and see people who incline to extremes, who are fanatical. We may be sure that this class of people do not understand the gospel. They have forgotten, if they ever knew, that it is very unwise to take a fragment of truth and treat it as if it were the whole thing" (*Gospel Doctrine,* 122). On another occasion President Smith taught: "Brethren and sisters, don't have [gospel] hobbies. Hobbies are dangerous in the Church of Christ. They are dangerous because they give undue prominence to certain principles or ideas to the detriment and dwarfing of others just as important, just as binding, just as saving as the favored doctrines or commandments.

"Hobbies give to those who encourage them a false aspect of the gospel of the Redeemer; they distort and place out of harmony its principles and teachings. The point of view is unnatural. Every principle and practice revealed from God is essential to man's salvation, and to place any one of them unduly in front, hiding and dimming all others is unwise and dangerous; it jeopardizes our salvation, for it darkens our minds and beclouds our understandings" (*Gospel Doctrine,* 116–17).

True excellence in gospel living—compliance with the established laws and ordinances in a quiet and patient manner—results in humility, in greater reliance upon God, and in a broadening love and acceptance of one's fellow man.

One final matter associated with living by every word of God is the need on our part to stay current and up to date on prophetic counsel. This means, of course, that we must constantly be reading and listening and learning, attending with great earnestness to what the apostles and prophets in our day are saying. We have persons in the Church today who know very well what Joseph Smith or Brigham Young taught but who have not paid the price to keep their learning and their testimony current. President Harold B. Lee offered sobering counsel when he taught:

"Years ago as a young missionary I visited Nauvoo and Carthage with my mission president, and we were holding a missionary meeting in the jail room where Joseph and Hyrum had met their deaths. The mission president related the historical events that led up to the martyrdom and then he closed with this very significant statement: 'When the Prophet Joseph Smith was martyred, there were many saints who died spiritually with Joseph.' So it was when Brigham Young died: so it was when John Taylor died. Do revelations given to President John Taylor, for example, have any more authority than something that comes from our president and prophet today? . . . We have some today willing to believe someone who is dead and gone and to accept his words as having more authority than the words of a living authority today" (*Stand Ye in Holy Places,* 153).

We build upon a foundation laid by the Prophet Joseph Smith and the revelations and heavenly powers communicated to him. Joseph Smith stands in a singular position to the Latter-day Saints: our worship is reserved for the members of the Godhead, but a special form of respect and loyalty is extended to Brother Joseph. He is the head of a dispensation,

what might be called a prophet's prophet. In a magnificent
address delivered to the Church at the April 1916 general conference, President Joseph F. Smith spoke of the vital link between Joseph Smith, the founder of the faith, and the current
Church and its leaders: "I feel sure that the Prophet Joseph
Smith and his associates, who, under the guidance and inspi-
ration of the Almighty, and by his power, began this latter-
day work, would rejoice and do rejoice, if they are permitted
to look down upon the scene in this tabernacle. And I believe
they do have the privilege of looking down upon us, just as the
all-seeing eye of God beholds every part of his handiwork. . . .

"So, I feel quite confident that the eyes of Joseph the
Prophet, and of the martyrs of this dispensation, and of
Brigham and John and Wilford, and those faithful men who
were associated with them in their ministry upon the earth,
are carefully guarding the interests of the Kingdom of God
in which they labored and for which they strove during their
mortal lives. I believe they are as deeply interested in our wel-
fare today, if not with greater capacity with far more interest
behind the veil, than they were in the flesh. . . . And I have a
feeling in my heart that I stand in the presence not only of
the Father and the Son, but in the presence of those whom
God commissioned, raised up, and inspired, to lay the foundations of the work in which we are engaged" (*Messages of the
First Presidency,* 5:5–6).

And yet we readily acknowledge that ours is a forward-
looking Church; we do not dwell constantly upon what was
done in the past or even on how it was done. "The Lord, in
his infinite wisdom and goodness," Elder Bruce R. McConkie

explained, "knows what ought to be done with his servants. The other thing to note is that when the Lord calls a new prophet he does it because he has a work and a labor and a mission for the new man to perform.

"I can suppose," he continued, "that when the Prophet Joseph Smith was taken from this life the Saints felt themselves in the depths of despair. To think that a leader of such spiritual magnitude had been taken from them! . . . And yet when he was taken the Lord had Brigham Young. Brigham Young stepped forth and wore the mantle of leadership. With all respect and admiration and every accolade of praise resting upon the Prophet Joseph, *still Brigham Young came forward and did things that then had to be done* in a better way than the Prophet Joseph could have done them" ("Succession in the Presidency," 5; emphasis added).

We live by every word of God as we search the scriptures daily and see to it that we are comfortable and familiar with all four books in our standard works; as we listen attentively and study carefully the words of the Brethren, noting particularly how they offer prophetic commentary on scriptural passages and what divine direction they offer to the living Church; as we open ourselves to the promptings, guidance, and sanctifying power of the Spirit of God by living righteously, praying earnestly, and quietly meditating and pondering. No, man does not live by bread alone, nor does he live by money or fame or educational attainment alone; individuals survive and thrive spiritually as they learn to live by every word of God. Holders of the Melchizedek Priesthood acquire power in the priesthood as they search out, discover, and delight in what the Lord their God would have them be and do. Truly, "this greater priesthood administereth the gospel and holdeth the key of the mysteries of the kingdom, even the key of the knowledge of God" (D&C 84:19).

May we open ourselves to those sublime truths that a gracious Lord delights to grant unto his faithful servants.

POINTS TO PONDER

1. Jesus explained to Satan that man could not live "by bread alone, but by every word that proceedeth out of the mouth of God" (Matthew 4:4). What does that passage of scripture mean?

2. In what ways are we prone to be selectively obedient? How does that compare with keeping God's commandments with exactness?

3. Why do members of the Church occasionally fall into the trap of developing gospel hobbies? How may we avoid such attitudes and behaviors?

4. The leaders of the Church have counseled the Saints to live a balanced life and to stay in the mainstream of the Church. What do you suppose they mean by this counsel?

SANCTIFIED AND RENEWED

WE ARE TOLD IN THE REVELATION that sets forth the terms and conditions of the oath and covenant of the priesthood that if we obtain the priesthood and magnify our callings therein, we are "sanctified by the Spirit unto the renewing of [our] bodies" (D&C 84:33).

What does that mean? What does it mean to be sanctified? What is the relationship between magnifying a calling and being sanctified?

In a revelation given through the Prophet Joseph Smith at the time of the organization of the restored Church, the Lord explained: "And we know that all men must repent and believe on the name of Jesus Christ, and worship the Father in his name, and endure in faith on his name unto the end, or they cannot be saved in the kingdom of God. And we know that justification through the grace of our Lord and Savior Jesus Christ is just and true; and we know also, that sanctification through the grace of our Lord and Savior Jesus Christ is just and true, to all those who love and serve God with all their mights, minds, and strength" (D&C 20:29–31). It was as if the Master were saying he is well aware of the teachings of many of the churches in this day, and he would inform us that there is indeed a true doctrine of justification and sanctification, one that reflects things as they really are. That doctrine is found throughout the scriptures of the Restoration.

Justification is a legal term used in a scriptural context to describe one's relationship to God. To justify is to acquit, to vindicate, to pronounce righteous or innocent. In the gospel sense, one is justified when one is forgiven of one's sins and placed in a right relationship with God. That person is no longer under wrath or under condemnation but is now under the protective and liberating power of the Lord's atoning grace (see Romans 5:9; 8:1). That is, that person's position in regard to a holy God has been changed, been vastly improved. Thus, "being justified by faith, we have peace with God through our Lord Jesus Christ" (Romans 5:1).

Elder D. Todd Christofferson pointed out: "Pardon comes by the grace of Him who has satisfied the demands of justice by His own suffering, 'the just for the unjust, that he might bring us to God' (1 Peter 3:18). He removes our condemnation without removing the law. We are pardoned and placed in a condition of righteousness with Him. We become, like Him, without sin. We are sustained and protected by the law, by justice. We are, in a word, justified" (*Ensign,* June 2001, 20).

We are not justified by our own labors, no matter how noble and righteous they may be. In fact, Paul taught,

"Knowing that a man is not justified by the works of the law, but by the faith of Jesus Christ, even we have believed in Jesus Christ, that we might be justified by [our faith in] Jesus Christ, and not by the works of the law: for by the works of the law shall no flesh be justified" (Galatians 2:16; compare Romans 3:20; 2 Nephi 2:5).

Man's part of the gospel covenant is to exercise faith in the Savior, repent of his sins, receive the ordinances of salvation, and then agree to live a life befitting a new relationship with the Lord. "Given the magnitude of the gift of grace," Elder Christofferson explained, "we would never suppose, even with all the good we could possibly do in this life, that we had earned it. It is just too great. . . . It is, and will always be, in truth, the gift of God through His divine Son" (*Ensign,* June 2001, 22).

A Christian thinker not of our faith put it this way: "It is simply not the case that God does some of the work of our salvation and we have to do the rest. It is not the case that we begin by being justified by grace through faith and then have to go to work all by ourselves to complete the job by struggling, unaided, to live a holy life" (Wright, *After You Believe,* 60).

Paul reminded the early Saints at Rome that "all have sinned and come short of the glory of God, . . . being justified only by his grace through the redemption that is in Christ Jesus." Paul stated further, "Therefore we conclude that a man is justified by faith alone without the deeds of the law" (JST Romans 3:23–24, 28).

To be justified by God is to be made clean despite one's

inability to repay the master; it is to be declared innocent despite one's lack of moral perfection. It is to be acquitted from sin through one's faith in Christ, faith that manifests itself in faithfulness, including repentance and dedicated discipleship (see Romans 2:6–7, 13; Galatians 5:6; Titus 3:8, 14). The Lord compensates for the chasm between man's strivings and God's perfection, between where a man really is and where he must eventually be. But justification is both a journey and a destination, a process as well as a condition, and the heavens respond favorably toward the righteous desires of the heart, as though those desires were actualized. Man's direction is as vital as his immediate geography. "A comparison may be made," wrote Sidney B. Sperry, "to a man on an escalator. We anticipate that he will reach a given floor if he stays on the escalator. So a person will eventually be justified, but may be regarded as being so now, if he retains a remission of sins (Mosiah 4:26) and continually shows his faith in God" (*Paul's Life and Letters,* 176).

What then does it mean to be sanctified? We begin by acknowledging that the gospel is indeed the good news, the glad tidings, "that he came into the world, even Jesus, to be crucified for the world, and to bear the sins of the world, and to sanctify the world, and *to cleanse it from all unrighteousness*" (D&C 76:41; emphasis added). Christ came to make Saints of sinners, to open the way to holiness, to reconcile humankind to the Father, the "Man of Holiness" (Moses 6:57), and to lead back to the eternal presence all who would be led.

Just as Jesus is the only means by which people are justified, so is he the only means by which they are sanctified—cleansed, renewed, renovated, and lifted spiritually to the state best described as holiness. If to be justified is to be freed from sin, then to be sanctified is to be freed from the effects of sin. If justification describes one's new standing before Christ, sanctification describes one's state, the place of one's heart. Whereas one may be justified in a moment, at a specific point in time, such as when he or she receives baptism at the hands of legal administrators, or as he or she is granted forgiveness following a period of genuine repentance, sanctification is a process that goes on all of our days in mortality. As we receive and cultivate the gift of the Holy Ghost, as we do all in our power to maintain our worthiness to have the companionship of the Holy Ghost, the work of sanctification goes forward.

The Holy Ghost is the sanctifier, and it is his assignment to cleanse and purify the human soul, to burn the filth and dross from our hearts by fire. It is the Holy Spirit of God that erases carnality and brings us into a state of righteousness. Sanctification is a change of nature, a change of desire, a change not only of one's discipline but of one's disposition. Elder Orson Pratt explained that "the baptism of the Holy Ghost cannot be dispensed with by the believer, any more than the baptism of water. To be born of the water only justifies the sinner of past sins; but to be born, afterwards, of the Holy Ghost, sanctifies him and prepares him for spiritual blessings in this life, and for eternal life in the world to come" (*True Faith,* 13).

While I was serving as a stake president, it was my assignment, often a difficult one, to preside over disciplinary councils. To be sure, it was always a pleasant experience to witness the power of the mercy and grace of our beloved Redeemer in the lives of his Saints as they chose to repent of their sins and put their lives back together. There were times, however, when it was necessary, because of the severity of a transgression, to disfellowship or excommunicate persons from the Church. Because stake disciplinary councils are conducted primarily for holders of the Melchizedek Priesthood, it was my responsibility to oversee the proceedings of some difficult and extremely painful meetings when serious sin had been committed.

Within a couple of years I began to notice a pattern. In those cases where serious immorality on the part of the Melchizedek Priesthood holder was involved, I observed quite often that the man in transgression had been involved in similar transgressions prior to his service as a full-time missionary. We would inquire: "Tell us about your repentance before leaving for a mission." Often the comments would take the form of "Well, I stopped doing those things before I left." Then the more probing question on our part took the form of, "More specifically, tell us about the change of heart that you underwent. Would you describe it as a mighty change of heart?" There was inevitably a rather long and uncomfortable pause, followed by "I'm not sure I underwent a real change of heart. I just didn't allow myself to be immoral again before leaving for the mission field." It was a telling moment, and a great teaching moment, as well.

It is one thing to simply stop doing wrong—which, of course, is terribly important—and another thing entirely to undergo the kind of spiritual metamorphosis in which the sinner is truly changed, his desires and longings and ambitions transformed, his inclinations and disposition altered. That process is sanctification.

Elder B. H. Roberts offered an accurate description of the work of the Holy Spirit in sanctifying the human soul. He pointed out that the forgiven soul may still continue to "feel the force of sinful habits bearing heavily upon him. He who has been guilty of habitual untruthfulness, will at times find himself inclined, perhaps, to yield to that habit. He who has stolen may be sorely tempted, when opportunity arises, to steal again. While he who has indulged in licentious practices may again find himself disposed to give way to the seductive influence of the siren. So with drunkenness, malice, envy, covetousness, hatred, anger, and in short all the evil dispositions that flesh is heir to.

"There is *an absolute necessity for some additional sanctifying grace that will strengthen the poor human nature,* not only to enable it to resist temptation, but also to root out from the heart concupiscence—the blind tendency or inclination to evil. The heart must be purified, every passion, every propensity made submissive to the will, and the will of man brought into subjection to the will of God.

"*Man's natural powers are unequal to this task*; so, I believe, all will testify who have made the experiment. Mankind stand in some need of a strength superior to any they possess of themselves, to accomplish this work of rendering pure our fallen nature. *Such strength, such power, such a sanctifying grace is conferred on man in being born of the Spirit*—in receiving the

Holy Ghost. Such, in the main, is its office, its work" (*Gospel and Man's Relationship to Deity*, 169–70; emphasis added).

This two-stage process of spiritual change is quite clear in scripture. John the Beloved wrote: "If we confess our sins, he is faithful and just *to forgive us our sins*, and *to cleanse us of all unrighteousness*" (1 John 1:9; emphasis added).

Similarly, the people of Benjamin, having heard the powerful message of their great king, cried out: "O have mercy, and apply the atoning blood of Christ that we may receive forgiveness of our sins, and *our hearts may be purified*; for we believe in Jesus Christ, the Son of God, who created heaven and earth and all things; who shall come down among the children of men" (Mosiah 4:2; emphasis added).

Truly, the one who is worthy to ascend unto the hill of the Lord, worthy of the temple here and paradise hereafter, is "he that hath clean hands, and *a pure heart*" (Psalm 24:3–4; emphasis added).

Now, what is the relationship between magnifying our calling in the priesthood and being "sanctified by the Spirit unto the renewing of [our] bodies"? For one thing, when we magnify our callings, we are focused on the work of the Lord and on the one thing God loves the most—his sons and daughters. One who magnifies his calling has chosen to put aside his own preferences, his own convenience, his own agenda, and to rivet himself on the work of God's kingdom. At a time of great challenge in Nephite history, a day when many of the people of the Church of Jesus Christ were consumed with pride, another group of Saints made a decision that mattered and thus made it a moment that mattered. "They did fast and pray oft, and did wax stronger and stronger in their humility, and firmer and firmer in the faith of Christ, unto the filling their souls with joy and consolation, yea, even to the purifying and the sanctification of their hearts, *which sanctification cometh because of their yielding their hearts unto God*" (Helaman 3:35; emphasis added).

We yield our hearts unto God when we concede, surrender, relinquish, render to the Almighty our hopes and dreams, our wants and desires, our ambitions and longings. We yield our hearts unto God when we gladly acknowledge that we are incapable of doing with our lives all that could be done by God, if we were to allow him to be in charge.

To yield our hearts unto God, which enables him to begin to sanctify us, is the same thing as having "an eye single to the glory of God" (D&C 4:5; 82:19). It is to be fixed and focused, consecrated and aligned, even righteously obsessed with what the Lord wants done. It is to have a ready resolve to do things his way, a constant prayer in our hearts to see things the way he does, to feel toward things as he does. The Savior explained, "The light of the body is the eye: if therefore thine eye be single, thy whole body shall be full of light" (Matthew 6:22). Or, as the promise is spelled out more completely in modern revelation, "And if your eye be single to my glory, your whole bodies shall be filled with light, and there shall be no darkness in you; and that body which is filled with light comprehendeth all things" (D&C 88:67).

While the King James language (in the Bible as well as in the Doctrine and Covenants) is that our eye should be single, other translations render this expression as "if your eye is clear" (New American Standard Bible), "if your eye is healthy" (New Revised Standard Version), "if your eyes are good" (New International Version), and "if your eyes are sound" (Revised English Bible). Surely to have our eyes or minds single to God's glory is spiritually sound, good, and healthy, resulting in the clearest vision of truth, even a "knowledge of things as they are, and as they were, and as they are to come" (D&C 93:24; compare Jacob 4:13). Indeed, to will one thing—God's thing, so to speak—is to open ourselves to his purposes and his perspective, to gain, as Paul taught, "the mind of Christ" (1 Corinthians 2:16). And accompanying his perspective is always his cleansing and enabling power.

In speaking of priesthood holders from ancient times and specifically those who labored with the righteous king Melchizedek, Alma said: "Now, as I said concerning the holy order, or this high priesthood, there were many who were ordained and became high priests of God; and it was on account of their exceeding faith and repentance, and their righteousness before God, they choosing to repent and work righteousness rather than to perish; *therefore they were called after this holy order, and were sanctified,* and their garments were washed white through the blood of the Lamb. Now they, *after being sanctified by the Holy Ghost,* having their garments made white, being pure and spotless before God, *could not look upon sin save it were with abhorrence*; and there were many, exceedingly great many, who were made pure and entered into the rest of the Lord their God" (Alma 13:10–12; emphasis added).

Now what of the language of the Lord that those who magnify their callings are "sanctified by the Spirit unto the renewing of their bodies"? (D&C 84:33). With faithfulness in our duties comes a quickening, a spiritual animation, a zest or energy or dynamism that we know to be the Master's enabling power. In other words, as we are true and faithful to our covenants, which would include being dutiful and obedient, Christ extends his power and his strength to us. The apostle Paul wrote: "I am crucified with Christ: nevertheless I live; yet not I, but Christ liveth in me"—that is, It isn't merely my self-generated, will-powered life but rather Christ's life, extended to me as a gracious gift—"and the life which I now live in the flesh I live by [my faith in] the Son of God, who loved me, and gave himself for me" (Galatians 2:20). Notice how Paul put it years later: "Now the God of peace, that brought again from the dead our Lord Jesus, that great shepherd of the sheep, through the blood of the everlasting covenant, make you perfect in every good work to do his will, *working in you that which is well pleasing in his sight,* through Jesus Christ" (Hebrews 13:20–21; emphasis added; compare Philippians 2:12–13).

In describing the sanctified man, Elder Parley P. Pratt explained: "His mind is quickened, his intellectual faculties are aroused to intense activity. He is, as it were, illuminated. He learns more of divine truth in a few days than he could have learned in a lifetime in the best merely human institutions of the world.

"His affections are also purified, exalted, and increased in proportion. He loves his Heavenly Father and Jesus Christ with a perfect love. He also loves the members of the Church, or the body of Christ, as he loves his own soul. . . . He would make any sacrifice that might be expedient to do good. He would lay down his life most cheerfully, without one moment's hesitation or regret, if required of him by the cause of truth" (*Key to the Science of Theology*, 59–60).

Such a man is driven and directed by covenant, by a sacred cooperation with Deity toward the sanctification of the soul. Thus "men and women who turn their lives over to God, will discover that He can make a lot more out of their lives than they can. He will deepen their joys, expand their vision, quicken their minds, strengthen their muscles, lift their spirits, multiply their blessings, increase their opportunities, comfort their souls, raise up friends, and pour out peace. Whoever will lose his life in the service of God will find eternal life" (*Teachings of Ezra Taft Benson*, 361).

Truly, that same Spirit that sanctifies us from sin, that accompanies dedicated discipleship, is the Spirit that brings about a newness of soul, a lightness of spirit, an excitement with mortality, a fascination with the works and ways of the Master. As we read the scriptures, "new writing" (1 Nephi 16:29) appears everywhere, while the simplest and most basic doctrines begin to take on a profundity that we never would have supposed; in short, we begin to see things with new eyes and to feel things with a new heart. We put off our old ways of viewing things and acquire what the scriptures call the "eye of faith" (Alma 5:15; 32:40; Ether 12:19). We gain a deeper sensitivity to right and wrong; enjoy greater manifestations of the gift of discernment; develop more educated and refined desires; and feel a deeper compassion for those who mourn or suffer or reach out for succor. This "quickening in the inner man" (Moses 6:65) peels away the film and façade of sin, makes unnecessary the rigors and taxing labors of ostentation and superfluity, and empowers us to sift out the sordid and the subsidiary. We find ourselves much less interested in laboring in secondary causes but, on the other hand, have a consuming yet patient passion to occupy ourselves with that which brings light and life and love. We treasure the simple pleasures in life and rejoice in the goodness of our God. With us, as with the future transfigured earth, all things will have become new (see Revelation 21:5; D&C 101:25).

POINTS TO PONDER

1. What do the scriptures mean when they speak of a person being justified? How does this justification come about?

2. What does it mean to be sanctified?

3. What is the relationship between magnifying our callings and being sanctified?

4. How does faithfully carrying out our responsibilities result in a renewal of our bodies?

SONS OF THE PROPHETS

MY FATHER WAS A HARD WORKER and a busy man, someone who, between occupational demands and Church responsibilities, seemed always to be on the run. And there were many times when he asked me to accompany him. One of the things I noticed very early was how people, men and women of other faiths as well as Latter-day Saints, loved Dad. Dad was a respected man, one who was painfully honest and, unfortunately, kind enough to be taken advantage of many, many times. I know for a fact that he co-signed on probably ten different automobiles for people who asked him to assist them in making a purchase, and in at least five of those cases the people skipped town and left Dad with the bill to pay. As I got a little older, I remember asking him why he allowed people to do that to him.

"Well, son," he replied in essence, "nobody likes to be cheated, but I refuse to be cynical about my fellowman and to assume that every person I meet is out to get me. I won't live that way, and I wouldn't want to live in a world that is filled with that kind of mistrust. I'd rather assume the best and trust people, knowing that once in a while people will take advantage of you." That's the kind of man he was. He was trusted, and he was greatly loved.

I always enjoyed it when individuals, once they heard my name and learned where I was from, would ask, "Are you Lou's boy?" (Dad's name was Albert Louis, but most people called him Lou.)

Once I acknowledged that I was, the compliments and praise of Dad would begin to flow. When I was a junior in high school, my American history class was taught by Mr. Meares, a man who had played high school football with my father years before. Once he found out who I was, he did two things: he always called me Lou; and he made me his pet, his preferred student. That year only two new history textbooks were available, and the forty or so others were worn and tattered. I was one of two students to get a new copy.

Now, I didn't do anything to earn the perks or receive the benefits I was given in that class except be the son of Lou Millet. Well, let's just say that I never complained about being the teacher's pet. I loved it. I loved being my father's son, and that alone gave me a feeling of self-worth—as well as a firm resolve to be all that my father thought I was, especially in moments of temptation.

In the first century after Christ, Timothy was a young man who was in a situation not unlike the one I was in as a young man. Timothy's grandmother Lois and his mother, Eunice, had become converts to Christianity (see 2 Timothy 1:5; see also Acts 16:1), and Timothy's family seems to have been from Lystra or Derbe, cities where Paul preached on his first missionary journey (see Acts 14). Timothy himself became a beloved missionary companion to the apostle Paul, who often spoke of Timothy affectionately: "Unto Timothy, my own son in the faith [meaning "my true son in the faith"]: Grace, mercy, and peace, from God our Father and Jesus Christ our Lord" (1 Timothy 1:2; see also v. 18; 2 Timothy 1:2; Philippians 2:19–22; 1 Corinthians 4:14–17). In the days of Elijah and Elisha, a group of young men who were receiving spiritual training became known as the "sons of the prophets" (2 Kings 2:5). The two thousand stripling warriors were likewise called the sons of Helaman (see Alma 56:10).

And so it is with those of us who have been ordained to the priesthood in the dispensation of the fulness of times. We have received the Aaronic Priesthood, which is a preparatory order, a sort of training division of the priesthood. This lesser priesthood prepares us for the greater priesthood, "the Holy Priesthood, after the Order of the Son of God" (D&C 107:3). We are instructed in the revelation that sets forth the terms and conditions of the covenant of the priesthood that "whoso is faithful unto the obtaining of these two priesthoods of which I have spoken, and the magnifying their calling, are sanctified by the Spirit unto the renewing of their bodies. They become *the sons of Moses and of Aaron and the seed of Abraham*" (D&C 84:33–34; emphasis added). Moses and Aaron were notable priesthood leaders in their day, just as Abraham had been in his day. Because the priesthoods of Moses and Aaron, the Melchizedek and the Aaronic respectively, bless the lives of individuals everywhere, the Lord has chosen to call his faithful priesthood holders the sons of Moses and Aaron, adopted into their families as it were, no matter what their actual lineage may be. In speaking specifically of the lesser priesthood, one writer put it this way: "The literal descendants of Moses and Aaron are Levites. But the Lord was not talking [in D&C 84:34] about their literal descendants; he was talking about those who are 'faithful unto the obtaining these two priesthoods'; these are they who 'become the sons of Moses and of Aaron.' Levites, by adoption, without regard to lineal descent" (Palmer, *Aaronic Priesthood,* 319–20).

Because Moses the Lawgiver was not a gifted speaker and did not feel comfortable in that role, Jehovah appointed Aaron to be his spokesman (see Exodus 4:10–16; JST Genesis 50:34–35). Moses was the prophet or spokesman for Deity, but Aaron was the man called to deliver those words directly to the children of Israel. In an interesting way, each of us as an Aaronic or Melchizedek Priesthood holder is called by God to be a spokesman. In our respective assignments and under the direction of those who hold the keys, we are to "stand as witnesses of God at all times and in all things, and in all places that [we] may be in, even until death" (Mosiah 18:9). We are charged, with Elder Thomas B. Marsh, to "declare glad tidings," to "declare the things which have been revealed to [the Lord's] servant Joseph Smith, Jun." (D&C 31:4; compare 33:8–10).

In our time, when the prophets and apostles have counseled us to hasten the work of salvation, it is incumbent upon the elders and high priests of the Church to "let [our] preaching be the warning voice, every man to his neighbor in mildness and in meekness" (D&C 38:41; compare 88:81). In a broader way, we are to proclaim the sacred truths of the Restoration, "saying none other things than that which the prophets and apostles have written, and that which is taught [us] by the Comforter through the prayer of faith" (D&C 52:9; see also v. 36). Because the conferral of the Melchizedek Priesthood upon us entails a divine investiture of authority, when we speak under the influence of the Holy Ghost, our words are his words; it is as if the Lord had spoken. This is what Nephi meant when he referred to those who had received the Holy Ghost and enjoyed the baptism of fire and the privilege of speaking "with the tongue of angels," which is to speak the words of Christ (2 Nephi 31:13–14; 32:1–3). We are by that means spokesmen for the Almighty: He is our Principal, and we are his agents (see D&C 64:29).

Just as Moses was a lawgiver, one who received and then taught God's commandments to ancient Israel, so are we charged as Latter-day Saint priesthood holders to let our voice be heard—to stand up for righteousness and truth, defend our liberties, and hold tenaciously to those moral standards that have been the bedrock of our society for centuries. Today the shifting sands of secularity have resulted in an erosion of time-honored principles of goodness and decency, such that those who do have the courage to mention religion or religious values in the public square are not just disagreed with or even denounced but are ignored or marginalized.

As Professor Stephen L. Carter of the Yale Law School

pointed out, "One sees a trend in our political and legal cultures toward treating religious beliefs as arbitrary and unimportant, a trend supported by a rhetoric that implies that there is something wrong with religious devotion. More and more, our culture seems to take the position that believing deeply in the tenets of one's faith represents a kind of mystical irrationality, something that thoughtful, public-spirited American citizens would do better to avoid. . . . The consistent message of modern American society is that whenever the demands of one's religion conflict with what one has to do to get ahead, one is expected to ignore the religious demands and act . . . well . . . rationally." Carter points out that "one good way to end a conversation—or start an argument—is to tell a group of well-educated professionals that you hold a political position (preferably a controversial one, such as being against abortion or pornography) because it is required by your understanding of God's will. In the unlikely event that anyone hangs around to talk with you about it, the chances are that you will be challenged on the ground that you are intent on imposing your religious beliefs on other people. And in contemporary political and legal culture, nothing is worse" (*Culture of Disbelief,* 6–7, 13, 23).

Clearly our world is in need of many Moseses, many lawgivers, many upholders of the word and will of the Almighty. As Church leaders have emphasized recently, neither social consensus nor even civil law can annul a decree of God (see Oaks, *Ensign,* November 2013, 72–75; Andersen, *Ensign,* May 2014, 19–20).

Finally, both Moses and Aaron accepted responsibilities

that must have seemed overwhelming and perhaps even undoable. Aaron and his sons were called to initiate a new order of priesthood, a lesser priesthood that would administer a lesser gospel, an order of priesthood that would administer the preparatory gospel and its law of carnal commandments (see D&C 84:26–27); to hold the keys associated with the temple worship to be accomplished within the precincts of the Tabernacle and later the temples of Solomon, Zerubbabel, and Herod; to put in place an intricate system of sacrifices and offerings that went well beyond the simple sacrifice that Adam was commanded to perform (see Moses 5:5–8); and to preside over the detailed set of performances and ordinances that we know as the law of Moses (see Mosiah 13:30; 2 Nephi 25:30; Alma 25:15).

And what of Moses? We have already mentioned that he was called of God as a covenant spokesman but that he felt inadequate as a public speaker. Further, we simply cannot imagine the wear and tear, the toil and tears that must have come frequently to Moses as he sought to free Israel from Pharaoh's Egypt; to lead the people through the wilderness for forty years; to endure perpetual criticisms and complaints, the murmuring and madness of moving that many people—a people faced with fear and frailties, deserts and discouragement, hunger and hysteria—not only from Sinai to Canaan but also from Egyptian idolatry to the acceptance and worship of the Lord Jehovah. A superhuman task, to be sure, but a job that was done through supernatural intervention.

My point is simply that Moses and Aaron felt inadequate

and ill-suited to magnify their callings, just as you and I feel when we are called to serve in positions that may frighten us and certainly stretch us, duties that drive us to our knees in a solemn effort to gain the spirit of our calling. We are the sons of Moses and Aaron, and we are called, to some extent at least, to walk in their shoes and follow their lead.

The revelation states that those who magnify their callings become "the seed of Abraham" (D&C 84:34). But aren't most all of us as Latter-day Saints the seed of Abraham already? Do not our patriarchal blessings so signify? Yes, most Latter-day Saints are physical descendants of the great father of the faithful, although some are adopted into the house of Israel at the time of their baptism. We must ever remember, however, as Paul taught, that "they are not all Israel, which are of Israel" (Romans 9:6). As important as it is to be linked genealogically to Abraham, Isaac, and Jacob and to be a part of the chosen people, it is even more important to have come unto Jesus Christ by faith, repented of our sins, received the ordinances of salvation and exaltation, and remained true and faithful to our covenants (see 2 Nephi 30:1–2).

In other words, one is not truly of the seed of Abraham who is not also of the seed of Christ (see Mosiah 15:10–13)— one who has been born again, been transformed by his blood, become a new creation of the Holy Spirit (see 2 Corinthians 5:17; Galatians 6:15; Ephesians 4:24; Mosiah 27:24–26), been adopted into the family of Christ, and taken upon oneself the name of Jesus Christ and honored and reverenced that name through personal fidelity and devotion (see Mosiah 5:7–8; 27:23–26).

"For as many of you as have been baptized into Christ," Paul wrote, "have put on Christ. There is neither Jew nor Greek, there is neither bond nor free, there is neither male nor female: for ye are all one in Christ Jesus. And *if ye be Christ's, then are ye Abraham's seed, and heirs according to the promise*" (Galatians 3:27–29; emphasis added). To enter into the gospel covenant and to accept the Mediator of that covenant, the Lord Jesus Christ, is to be welcomed into the Savior's family. And to be adopted into the family of the Holy One of Israel is to secure one's place within the family of the grandfather of Israel, that is, to become the seed of Abraham.

To be of the seed of Abraham is to be willing to walk where father Abraham walked, to gain the eternal perspective of Abraham, and to be willing to observe our covenants by sacrifice (see D&C 97:8). Abraham says of himself: "I sought for the blessings of the fathers, and the right whereunto I should be ordained to administer the same; having been myself a follower of righteousness, desiring also to be one who possessed great knowledge, and *to be a greater follower of righteousness,* and *to possess a greater knowledge,* and to be a father of many nations, a prince of peace, and *desiring to receive instructions,* and to keep the commandments of God, I became a rightful heir, a High Priest, holding the right belonging to the fathers" (Abraham 1:2; emphasis added).

Do we get the picture? Can we glimpse the heart of Abraham, that magnificent priesthood holder? Abraham wanted to know more than he then knew, and he wanted to be more than he was. Further, he desired to receive instructions. He was open to counsel, eager for divine insight, ripe for promptings and guidance. Our Father in Heaven will move heaven and earth to bless such a man and will cause that person's life and daily walk to flourish. This is what the Brethren in recent years have referred to as real growth, meaning deep conversion and unconditional consecration. In this as in many things, Abraham is our model, our spiritual father.

One final thought about our being the seed of Abraham. We remember that to Abraham, as well as to his sons Isaac and Jacob, Jehovah declared: "I will make thy seed as the dust of the earth: so that if a man can number the dust of the earth, then shall thy seed also be numbered" (Genesis 13:16; see also 15:5–6; 28:14). In other words, Abraham was promised, in what we call the Abrahamic covenant, that his posterity would be given the gospel, the priesthood, and eternal life, or more correctly, eternal lives, meaning the continuation of the family unit into eternity (see D&C 132:19–20, 24; Abraham 2:8–11).

Just as Abraham was the father of the faithful in his day, so in our day Joseph Smith the Prophet may be considered to be a father of the faithful. As a result of the keys of the priesthood having been restored to Joseph Smith through the ministrations of Moses, Elias, and Elijah in the Kirtland Temple (see D&C 110), all of the blessings of the ancients, including the Abrahamic covenant and the supernal rights and privileges of the holy temple, have come into our dispensation. The Master taught Joseph the Seer: "And as I said unto Abraham concerning the kindreds of the earth, even so

I say unto my servant Joseph: In thee and in thy seed shall all the kindred of the earth be blessed" (D&C 124:58). Later the Prophet was taught in the revelation on eternal marriage: "Abraham received promises concerning his seed, and of the fruit of his loins—from whose loins ye are, namely, my servant Joseph—which were to continue so long as they were in the world; and as touching Abraham and his seed, out of the world they should continue; both in the world and out of the world should they continue as innumerable as the stars. . . . This promise is yours also, because ye are of Abraham, and the promise was made unto Abraham; and by this law is the continuation of the works of my Father, wherein he glorifieth himself" (D&C 132:30–31).

What is true of Abraham and of Joseph Smith is true also of you and me. We may also, within our own righteous sphere of influence, become fathers of the faithful. "When he is married in the temple for time and all eternity," Elder Bruce R. McConkie explained, "each worthy member of the Church enters personally into the same covenant the Lord made with Abraham. This is the occasion when the promises of eternal increase are made, and it is then specified that those who keep the covenants made there shall be inheritors of all the blessings of Abraham, Isaac, and Jacob" (*New Witness,* 508). Being the children of Christ, we are also the children of Abraham in the fullest and most complete sense of that promise.

As we magnify our callings in the priesthood, we place ourselves in good company, in the blessed company of those past and present whose dedication to duty and whose commitment to covenants was sure and solid and enduring. We are members of the royal family.

POINTS TO PONDER

1. What is the value of a good name? Why is it so important to labor to keep that good name?

2. Who are the sons of Moses and Aaron?

3. Who are the seed of Christ, meaning the spiritual sons and daughters of Christ?

4. Who are the seed of Abraham? Why would we want to bear honorably the name of Father Abraham?

THE ELECT OF GOD

WORDS SUCH AS *chosen, elect,* and even *church* are used in more than one way in scripture. Let's first consider the word *chosen.*

A good friend of mine named Richard, a wonderful man not of our faith, described to me an experience he had while visiting the city of Jerusalem. He had started his tour of the Holy Land in Galilee and worked his way south over the next ten days. This particular day he had arrived in Jerusalem and visited the Western Wall, known also as the Wailing Wall, which is all that remains of a retaining wall on the western side of the Temple Mount. He wondered why the place had come to be known as the Wailing Wall, since everywhere he looked, he beheld joy and gladness. Three different families had just celebrated the bar mitzvah of their twelve-year-old sons, the rite of passage by which the boys became men, a "son of the law" or "son of the commandment." My friend commented on what a profound effect these celebrations had had on him and spoke admiringly of a ceremony that seemed to be so much more than a quaint custom. He lingered until most of the celebrating parties had left.

At that point Richard was able to focus his attention more directly on the wall itself and on what was taking place there. Everywhere he looked he saw men standing right up against the wall, many of them swaying forward and backward, reading their Torah, praying, obviously deep in contemplative study and meditation. He made his way closer to the wall and put on one of the paper head coverings that were provided. Now, you need to understand that my friend doesn't have a shy bone in his body and is absolutely fearless when it comes to doing new things or striking up conversations with total strangers. True to his nature, Richard walked up to a gentleman at the wall, said, "Excuse me, sir," and waited for a response.

The man turned around with a look of frustration and said, rather harshly, "What is it?"

Richard blurted out, "Why is this place called the Wailing Wall?"

The man replied with a question: "You are a visitor to this place?"

"Yes," Richard responded, "and I'm trying to understand what's going on here."

The gentleman's countenance changed and appeared much more cordial, more willing to be helpful. He said, "It is a place where Jews come to grieve, to mourn, to reflect soberly on those awful occasions when the temples here were destroyed, the city sacked, our people oppressed by nation after nation."

Richard was touched by the man's kindness and said, "Thank you so much. That's extremely helpful."

The man at the wall smiled and nodded, turned around, and resumed his prayers.

Richard explained to me that at this point he felt like an intruder, someone who simply didn't belong there. But that moment of reticence was quick in passing. He stepped closer to the man at the wall and said, "Excuse me. I have another question."

The man turned about the second time, evidencing a bit less frustration than the first time, but he was still slightly bothered. "Yes, how can I help?"

Richard answered: "I don't know much about the Jews or Jewish history. I have obviously heard about the Holocaust and about the formation of the state of Israel. I know that the Arab-Israeli conflict has been going on for a long time. But my question is simply this: For as long as I can remember, I have heard the Jewish people referred to as God's chosen people. What does that mean? It seems to me that you have had tragedy and pain and sorrow forever. How is it that you folks are the chosen people? What is it that you are chosen to do?"

My friend told me that the man's brow furrowed, his eyes moistened, and his gaze took on a rather distant, mystical look. After what Richard described as a painful pause, the man looked up humbly and said, "Well, that's a wonderful question, a deep one. I suppose . . . I suppose that we are chosen . . . chosen to suffer." The man nodded ever so kindly and returned to his worship.

My friend related that he spent the rest of the day in solemn contemplation himself.

Obviously the Jews are chosen to do more than suffer, but they have certainly had more than their share of that. As Latter-day Saints who take the Old Testament seriously, who look to the Book of Mormon and to modern revelation for answers, we know something about the doctrine of chosen-ness because we know something about the destiny of Israel. We know also that the Jews are not the only people designated as the Lord's chosen people. In other words, the definition of what it means to be chosen may vary dramatically, depending on the day, the time, the context.

So it is with the word *elect*. Who are the elect of God? We know that those who come to earth as members of the house of Israel had exercised "exceedingly great faith" in our first estate (Moroni 10:11), thus entitling themselves to a tabernacle of flesh through a royal lineage. They also come to earth with a sensitivity, a proclivity, an inclination to recognize and receive the truth when they encounter it. The early brethren referred to this as "believing blood" (McConkie, *New Witness,* 38).

The first missionaries of this dispensation were instructed: "And ye are called to bring to pass the gathering of mine elect; for mine elect hear my voice and harden not their hearts" (D&C 29:7). The Savior taught his meridian Twelve that his sheep follow him, the Good Shepherd, for they know his voice (see John 10:4). These are they who "humble themselves without being compelled to be humble; or rather, in other words, . . . [believe] in the word of God, and [are] baptized without stubbornness of heart, yea, without being brought to know the word, or even compelled to know, before they will believe" (Alma 32:16).

Now let's take the word *elect* to another level. The Prophet Joseph Smith taught that after we have come into the restored gospel, received and begun to cultivate the gift and gifts of the Holy Ghost, decided once and for all that it is the kingdom of God or nothing, and determined upon a course to serve God at all hazards, then we will eventually find our calling and election made sure (see www .josephsmithpapers.org, *Report of Instructions,* 17–19; *History, 1838–1856,* vol. C-1, addenda, 8–9; *John Taylor,* 219–28; see also *History of the Church,* 3:380).

That is, we will have passed the tests of mortality. It is as though the day of judgment had been advanced, that God had extended to us all that had been promised to the Saints of the Most High: salvation, eternal life, eternal lives, exaltation in the highest degree of the celestial kingdom—indeed, all that the Father has. In this grander sense, the elect of God are those who have made their calling and election sure and been sealed up unto eternal life.

The blessed assurance is that if we strive all our days to keep the covenants that we have made, including and especially the covenants of the temple and the covenant associated with receiving the Melchizedek Priesthood, we will come to know, either in this life or the next, that we will go on to receive the highest of eternal rewards. "If thou wilt do good, yea, and hold out faithful to the end, thou shalt be saved in the kingdom of God, which is the greatest of all the gifts of God; for there is no gift greater than the gift of salvation" (D&C 6:13; see also 14:7; 50:5; 58:2).

In this sacred context, we come face to face with another and higher use of the word *chosen*. We have been told in revelation that many are called but few are chosen (see D&C 121:34). Why is this? First, because they do not live up to the light and understanding they have been given but instead choose to walk earth's roads in the spiritual dawn when they could bask in the noonday sun (see D&C 95:5–6). Second, some of the called never grasp the eternal verity that "the rights of the priesthood are inseparably connected to the powers of heaven, and that the powers of heaven cannot be controlled nor handled only upon the principles of righteousness" (D&C 121:36).

In a revelation given through the Prophet Joseph Smith in June of 1834, we are told that "there has been a day of calling, but the time has come for a day of choosing; and let those be chosen that are worthy" (D&C 105:35). In offering inspired commentary on these words, Elder Bruce R. McConkie pointed out: "As is well known many are called to the Lord's work, but few are chosen for eternal life. So that those who are chosen may be sealed up unto eternal life, the scripture says: 'It shall be manifest unto my servant, by the voice of the Spirit, those that are chosen; and they shall be sanctified' (D&C 105:36). They are chosen by the Lord, but the announcement of their calling and election is delivered by the Spirit" (*New Witness*, 270).

It is interesting also to consider that there are different ways to speak of the Lord's Church. The Church of Jesus

Christ is the ecclesiastical organization made up of those who have received the message of the Restoration and the fulness of the gospel covenant; been baptized and confirmed by a legal administrator, an authorized bearer of the holy priesthood; and thus become a member of The Church of Jesus Christ of Latter-day Saints. The Church is that organized system established by revelation and directed by divine priesthood authority, given by a gracious God "for the perfecting of the saints, for the work of the ministry, for the edifying of the body of Christ: till we all come in the unity of the faith, and of the knowledge of the Son of God, unto a perfect man, unto the measure of the stature of the fulness of Christ" (Ephesians 4:11–13). Indeed, the Church of Jesus Christ, what might be called the outer church, has been provided as a defense and a refuge against the storms of the day (see D&C 115:6).

In the revelation that sets forth the terms and conditions of the oath and covenant of the Melchizedek Priesthood, the holy word proclaims that those men who obtain the priesthood and magnify their callings are sanctified and renewed: "They become the sons of Moses and of Aaron and the seed of Abraham, and *the church and kingdom,* and the elect of God" (D&C 84:33–34; emphasis added).

In commenting on the need for the people of God to be united, President Harold B. Lee stated: "The Saints might become one with the Father and the Son, spiritually begotten by baptism and through the Holy Ghost even unto the renewing of their bodies as the Lord tells us, and thus 'become the sons of Moses and of Aaron . . . the church and kingdom, and the elect of God' (D&C 84:34), and thus *become adopted into the holy family, the church and kingdom of God, the Church of the Firstborn"* (*Light of the World,* 49; emphasis added).

Those men who hold the priesthood and who choose the narrow path that leads to life eternal, thereby prepare themselves for sweet association with noble men and women on this side of the veil as well as sublime association with the elect on the other side of the veil. They eventually become members of the Church of the Firstborn, the inner church (beyond the veil of death) composed of men and women who have truly been born again (see D&C 93:21–22), have been sanctified from the sins and stains of Babylon, and have truly overcome the world (see D&C 76:53–54). These are they who have become what the scriptures call the sons and daughters of God: our Savior "came unto his own, and his own received him not. But as many as received him, to them gave he power to become the sons of God, even to them that believe on his name" (John 1:11–12; see also D&C 34:3).

Whereas baptism is the door into The Church of Jesus Christ of Latter-day Saints, the covenants and ordinances of the temple, particularly celestial marriage, open the door to membership in the Church of the Firstborn (see Smith, *Doctrines of Salvation,* 2:42). "They who dwell in his presence are the church of the Firstborn; and they see as they are seen, and know as they are known, having received of his fulness and of his grace" (D&C 76:94).

The Church of the Firstborn is the inner circle of faithful Saints who have proven true and faithful to their covenants. The Church of the Firstborn is the organized body of

Saints who qualify for full salvation. It is made up of those who qualify for the blessings of the Firstborn. Jesus is the Firstborn of the Father and as such is entitled to the birthright. As an act of consummate mercy and grace, our blessed Savior makes it possible for us to inherit, receive, and possess the same blessings he receives, as though we were the firstborn. Those who so qualify become heirs of God, joint-heirs or co-inheritors with Christ of all that the Father has, including eternal life (see Romans 8:17). "Wherefore, as it is written, they are gods, even the sons of God" (D&C 76:58). President Brigham Young, therefore, stated that "the ordinances of the house of God are expressly for the Church of the Firstborn" (*Journal of Discourses,* 8:154).

To have one's life and all the priesthood ordinances within that life "sealed unto them by the Holy Spirit of promise" is to have qualified to enjoy the highest benefits and blessings of the holy priesthood (D&C 132:19). "The power and authority of the higher, or Melchizedek Priesthood, is to hold the keys of all the spiritual blessings of the church—to have the privilege of receiving the mysteries of the kingdom of heaven"—those things that can only be received and comprehended by the power of God's Spirit—"to have the heavens opened unto them, to commune with the general assembly and church of the Firstborn, and to enjoy the communion and presence of God the Father, and Jesus the mediator of the new covenant" (D&C 107:18–19).

Now, to be sure, these are marvelous and unspeakable blessings, and we ought to know what's in store for those who endure faithfully to the end. But the attainment of such privileges will come to us only as we move forward spiritually, bit by bit, from precept to precept, from grace to grace. We will eventually qualify to dwell where God and Christ are and to be, in a measure, like them (see 1 John 3:1–3; Moroni 7:48), as we—

- Seek to be cleansed from all our sins and, once we have experienced that forgiveness, strive to retain a remission of sins from day to day (see Mosiah 4:11–12, 26).

- Attend to the solemn and sacred responsibilities we have to our wives and children, our home teaching families, and those persons beyond our immediate stewardship who could use our help.

- Develop a daily habit of personal devotion—prayer, scripture study, and contemplation of things of eternal import (see D&C 43:34).

- Make the holy temple a high priority in our life, as President Howard W. Hunter said, "the great symbol of [our] membership" (*Ensign*, October 1994, 2), so that we are rendering vicarious service to men and women who have passed through the veil of death, breathing in the spirit and power and calming influence of the house of the Lord, and transferring the spirit of the temple to our home.

- Stay worthy to officiate in priesthood ordinances and always look for opportunities to bless our brothers and sisters in our midst.

We hold the priesthood of our God. The authority to

officiate in his name has been conferred upon us. Through the power of his Spirit we can speak the words of Christ. God is our eternal Principal, and we are his agents. We are on his errand, and so whatever we do according to his will is his business (see D&C 64:29). We can and we must see to it that Jesus Christ, who is the great "Apostle and High Priest of our profession" (Hebrews 3:1), presides over every aspect of our lives. If this is our hope, our trust, and our focus, we and those we love will one day be invited into eternal glory and enjoy everlasting rest and what the scriptures call the fulness of the Father (D&C 76:20, 56; 84:24; 88:107; 93:4, 16, 19, 27; 132:6).

POINTS TO PONDER

1. What does it mean to be a chosen people?

2. What are the responsibilities of God's chosen people?

3. What does Doctrine and Covenants 29:7 teach us about becoming the elect of God?

4. What does it mean, in practical terms, for a person to make his or her calling and election sure? What is the Church of the Firstborn?

PRIESTS AND KINGS

WE ARE IN TRAINING HERE, in this life, for hereafter, the life to come. We are learning here in mortality how to operate within the parameters of God's holy priesthood. We now labor and oversee the work of the Almighty, namely, the salvation and exaltation of his children. In that glorious future day, we will continue that supernal endeavor, but we will do so as resurrected beings, having inherited "thrones, kingdoms, principalities, and powers, dominions" (D&C 132:19). That is the object and purpose of all we do in the Church and as holders of our Father's sacred authority.

We know that from the beginning of this dispensation, the Lord has directed his covenant people to build temples. And we know that those beloved early Saints built temples before they built church houses. What does that teach us? Is it not that the greatest and most sublime labors in which we can be involved on this earth are inextricably linked to the ordinances of the house of the Lord—baptisms for the dead, washings, anointings, endowments, and sealings? Is this not to impress upon our souls that the grandest and most transcendent work of all is the organization of eternal families and the perpetuation of the family unit into and throughout a neverending future? The Saints in Kirtland were commanded to build a temple, which they did with great earnestness and at untold sacrifice. The Lord there revealed to the Prophet Joseph Smith what we have come to call a partial endowment, and many of the leading brethren participated in washings, anointings, sealing of anointings, and the washing of feet (see Backman, *Heavens Resound*, 284–309). When the Latter-day Saints became established in their beautiful city of Nauvoo, the Lord called upon his people to come up higher. They were charged to "build a house to my name, for the Most High to dwell therein. For there is not a place found on earth that he may come to and restore again that which was lost unto you, or which he hath taken away, even the *fulness of the priesthood*" (D&C 124:27–28; emphasis added).

Let us reflect for a moment. John the Baptist had come on May 15, 1829, to restore the Aaronic Priesthood (see D&C 13). Peter, James, and John came in late May or early June 1829 to restore the Melchizedek Priesthood and the holy apostleship (see D&C 18:9; 27:12). Moses, Elias, and Elijah came to the Kirtland Temple on April 3, 1836, to restore the keys of the gathering of Israel, the ordinance of eternal marriage within the Abrahamic covenant, and the power to seal families forever (see D&C 110). In a letter written to the Nauvoo Saints dated September 6, 1842, Brother Joseph spoke of the coming of such prophets as Michael (Adam),

Peter, James, and John, Gabriel (Noah), Raphael, "and of divers angels, from Michael or Adam down to the present time, all declaring their dispensation, their rights, their keys, their honors, their majesty and glory, and the power of their priesthood" (D&C 128:21; see also v. 20).

That sounds like a pretty comprehensive list of angelic messengers who delivered keys, powers, and authorities to latter-day Israel. What else is there? What would the Lord mean when he referred to the "fulness of the priesthood" having been lost or taken away and thus needing to be restored?

President Gordon B. Hinckley explained that "the blessings of the temple represent that fulness of the priesthood of which the Lord spoke when He revealed His will unto the Prophet Joseph Smith. With the location of temples much nearer to the homes of our people, there is made more available to them all of the ordinances to be had in the Lord's house for both the living and the dead" (*Ensign,* May 2001, 5).

"If a man gets a fulness of the priesthood of God," the Prophet Joseph pointed out, "he has to get it in the same way that Jesus Christ obtained it, and that was by keeping all the commandments and obeying all the ordinances of the house of the Lord" (*Joseph Smith,* 419). President Joseph Fielding Smith offered this insight: "I do not care what office you hold in the Church—you may be an apostle, you may be a patriarch, a high priest, or anything else—but you cannot receive the fulness of the priesthood and the fulness of eternal reward unless you receive the ordinances of the house of the Lord" (Conference Report, April 1970, 58).

That is to say, men and women who become heirs of God and joint heirs with Christ must receive "the fulness of the ordinances of [God's] kingdom." Those who hold the fulness of the Melchizedek Priesthood "are kings and priests of the Most High God, holding the keys of power and blessings" (*Joseph Smith*, 419, 109). In other words, for a man or woman to receive the fulness of the priesthood is to be ordained a king or a queen, a priest or a priestess. And these blessings are to be had only within the house of the Lord.

God swore an oath to his Holy Son in these words: "The Lord hath sworn, and will not repent, Thou art a priest forever after the order of Melchizedek" (Psalm 110:4). Thus Jesus Christ has an unchangeable (perpetual or permanent) priesthood (see Hebrews 7:24). Or, as Alma explained concerning those who honor their priesthood, "they become high priests forever, after the order of the Son, the Only Begotten of the Father, who is without beginning of days or end of years, who is full of grace, equity, and truth" (Alma 13:9). Similarly, "all those who are ordained unto this priesthood are made *like unto the Son of God, abiding a priest continually*" (JST Hebrews 7:3–4; emphasis added). Truly, "even as the Father swears with an oath that his Son shall inherit all things through the priesthood, so he swears with an oath that all of us who magnify our callings in that same priesthood shall receive all that the Father hath" (Smith, Conference Report, October 1970, 92).

John the Revelator wrote of those who had kept the faith and thus qualified to receive the fulness of priesthood blessings—to be made kings and priests unto God forever (see

Revelation 5:9–10). In the vision of the glories, the Prophet Joseph Smith likewise beheld those who had become "priests and kings, who have received of his fulness and of his glory. . . . Wherefore, as it is written, they are gods, *even the sons of God*" (D&C 76:56–58; emphasis added).

Of such men we could say: they have honored the priesthood they bear; they have used the power of the Almighty to bless the lives of their own family and those over whom they have charge; they have been careful and dutiful agents of God, who is our divine Principal.

Much is made, particularly by critics of the Church, about the Latter-day Saint belief that men and women can become as God is. Although our Heavenly Father has not chosen to make known a great deal about this distinctive teaching, there are some things we do know. While the revelations declare that becoming like God is entailed in eternal life (see D&C 132:19–20), we do not believe we will ever, worlds without end, unseat or oust God the Eternal Father or his Only Begotten Son, Jesus Christ; those holy beings are and forever will be the Gods we worship. Even though we believe in the ultimate deification of men and women, I am unaware of any authoritative statement that suggests that we will ever worship any being other than the ones we worship now in the Godhead.

In describing those who are glorified and attain eternal life, Elder Parley P. Pratt stated: "The difference between Jesus Christ and another immortal and celestial man is this— the man is subordinate to Jesus Christ, does nothing in and of himself, but does all things in the name of Christ, and by his authority, being of the same mind, and ascribing all the glory to him and his Father" (*Key to the Science of Theology*, 21–22).

And what of some of the more colorful and creative descriptions of becoming like God that we occasionally hear bandied about, particularly by those of other faiths? The following statement appeared on the official Church Newsroom page at lds.org. It contained many of the most frequently-asked questions about our beliefs and practices:

"Question: Do Latter-day Saints believe that they will 'get their own planet'?"

The response: "No. This idea is not taught in Latter-day Saint scripture, nor is it a doctrine of the Church. This misunderstanding stems from speculative comments unreflective of scriptural doctrine. Mormons believe that we are all sons and daughters of God and that all of us have the potential to grow during and after this life to become like our Heavenly Father (see Romans 8:16–17). The Church does not and has never purported to fully understand the specifics of Christ's statement that 'in my Father's house are many mansions' (John 14:2)."

And so what does it mean to say that we may become like God? The vision states it simply: "Wherefore, as it is written, they are gods, *even the sons of God*" (D&C 76:58; emphasis added). The true sons of God are those who have confessed and forsaken their sins, enjoyed the cleansing power of Christ's atoning blood, been born again into the realm of divine experience, and acquired that power in the priesthood promised to the faithful. To be sure, we readily acknowledge that the chasm between a fallen, mortal being and an immortal, resurrected, and glorified Being is immense (see D&C 20:17; 109:77), but for Latter-day Saints who are true to their founding scriptures, to become like God—which to us really means to become more Christlike, more filled with the Spirit and the fruit of the Spirit (see Galatians 5:22–25)— is that goal toward which we press.

We do not believe we can work ourselves into glory or godhood or can gain eternal life through human effort alone. One does not become more and more Christlike through sheer grit and will power. Central to any and all spiritual progress is the atonement of Jesus Christ, and it is only by and through his righteousness that we may be declared righteous (see 2 Nephi 2:3). Only by the power of his precious blood may we be cleansed and sanctified from the taint and tyranny of sin. And it is only by and through the power of his everlasting life that we receive life—energy, strength, vitality, renewal, enabling power—to accomplish what we could never, worlds without end, accomplish on our own.

To summarize, we as Latter-day Saints teach that through the cleansing power of the blood of Jesus Christ and through the sanctifying power of the Holy Spirit, we may over time mature spiritually; we may, as our Eastern Orthodox friends would put it (and with which we would have no argument), partake of the energies, not the essence of God our Father.

Elder Hyrum Mack Smith, son of President Joseph F. Smith and a member of the Quorum of the Twelve Apostles, with his co-author Janne M. Sjodahl, commented on how sad it is that the critics of Mormonism "seem to think that they honor God by supposing that His children are infinitely inferior to Him. What kind of Father is He, then, that He should feel it an honor to be the progenitor of an inferior offspring? Is there a king on earth that would feel honored by having degenerates and beggars for children? Do not fathers and mothers rejoice in the progress of their children? Is it not their ambition to educate and train their loved ones, until these shall reach the highest possible degree of intelligence and efficiency? Surely, we can do no greater honor to God, our Father, than to admit the divine possibilities which He has implanted in His offspring, and which will be developed under His tuition in this life and hereafter, until His children are perfect as He is perfect" (*Doctrine and Covenants Commentary*, 826–27).

"The whole design of the gospel," President Gordon B. Hinckley declared, "is to lead us onward and upward to greater achievement, even, eventually, to godhood. This great possibility was enunciated by the Prophet Joseph Smith in the King Follett sermon and emphasized by President Lorenzo Snow. . . . Our enemies have criticized us for believing in this. Our reply is that this lofty concept in no way diminishes God the Eternal Father. He is the Almighty. He is the Creator and Governor of the universe. He is the greatest of all and will always be so. But just as any earthly father wishes for his sons and daughters every success in life, so I believe our Father in Heaven wishes for his children that they might approach him in stature and stand beside him resplendent in godly strength and wisdom" (*Ensign,* November 1994, 48). The discussion about our becoming as God is not a doctrinal detour. Rather, it is permanently linked with the highest of priesthood privileges, the greatest and grandest attainment of God's children through all the eternities.

It is important at this point, even vital, that we pause and make certain that we understand that the ultimate blessings associated with the oath and covenant of the priesthood cannot be received by a man alone. The highest blessings of the temple come to a man and a woman, husband and wife, together. President Charles W. Penrose stated that "when a woman is sealed to a man holding the Priesthood, she becomes one with him. . . . The glory and power and dominion that he will exercise when he has the fullness of the Priesthood and becomes a 'king and a priest unto God,' she will share with him" (Conference Report, April 1921, 24). For that matter, every woman in the Church can and should attend carefully to the word of the Lord concerning the oath and covenant of the priesthood. She should magnify her callings and enjoy the sanctifying and renewing powers of the Spirit as she does so; receive the Lord's servants and sustain them loyally; beware concerning herself; give diligent heed to the words of eternal life; live by every word of God; and, in general, be true and faithful to her covenants, particularly those covenants made in the house of the Lord. One who strives in this life to abide by these conditions, whether male or female, married or single, will in the life to come reap the everlasting rewards.

We are now on the path leading to life eternal, and we need to stay on that path. As noted earlier, we are in training here for what will come and what will be expected of us hereafter. Indeed, it is a rigorous training program through which God expects his sons to pass, and the Master does not apologize for requiring much of those to whom much has been given (see D&C 82:3). If we live in a manner that would allow the Holy Ghost to be a regular and eventually a constant companion (see D&C 121:46), then we will begin to learn the spirit of revelation and acquire those gifts and attributes that will bring unspeakable peace in this life and equip us to dwell comfortably and joyously with God and Christ and our eternal family in exaltation and glory. If we learn to lead and govern gently and lovingly in this life, we will have the opportunity to rule hereafter. John the Revelator beheld a sublime vision: "And I saw thrones, and they sat upon them, and judgment was given unto them. . . . Blessed and holy is he that hath part in the first resurrection: on such the second death hath no power, but they shall be *priests of God and of Christ, and shall reign with him* a thousand years" (Revelation 20:4, 6; emphasis added).

The revelations state that if in mortality we live in a manner to allow us to be "quickened by a portion of the celestial glory," we will, in the resurrection, "receive of the same even a fulness" (D&C 88:29). Exaltation will not, however, be a spiritual quantum leap in transforming us from a natural man to a spiritual man; there is a law of restoration spoken of by Alma (see Alma 41:10) and a law of the harvest spoken of by the apostle Paul (see Galatians 6:7–8). Let us acknowledge that we are not yet exactly where we need to be, or even where we want to be right now. But hopefully we are on the proper path, moving in the right direction, striving to be better. That direction is crucial, for we will continue in that same direction when we pass through the veil of death (see Alma 34:34). If we are striving to keep the Spirit of the Lord with us; to be the best husband and father we can be; to put out of our lives those things that distract, degrade, and eventually destroy; to fill our lives with light and life and goodness; to serve diligently in our priesthood callings, then we will continue to have that same spirit resting upon us when we die; we will enter the postmortal spirit world and continue in that same direction among men and women of like disposition. And it will be glorious!

It is in that spirit that I share a most profound statement from President Lorenzo Snow: "We expect in the resurrection," he said, "to exercise the powers of our priesthood—we can exercise them only in proportion as we secure its righteousness and perfections; these qualifications can be had only as they are sought and obtained, so that in the morning of the resurrection we will possess those acquisitions only which we secured in this world! *Godliness cannot be conferred but must be acquired*" ("Address to the Saints in Great Britain," 362; emphasis added).

Our charge is to acquire those qualities and attributes. The eternal compensation for whatever effort we expend will be more than worth the effort.

POINTS TO PONDER

1. What does it mean to say that we are in training here in preparation for hereafter?

2. What does it mean to say that we will be priests and kings forever? (see D&C 76:56).

3. What is the fulness of the priesthood? Where is it to be found?

4. What does it mean that we may become as God in the life to come? How does faithfully magnifying our callings in this life prepare us for becoming gods hereafter?

Conclusion

REFLECTIONS
AND RESOLUTIONS

THESE THINGS THAT WE HAVE CONSIDERED to this point are true, and they are real. We must ever and always look to the ideal, to that to which we aspire in the world to come. But we live for the time being in a world that is filled with evil, a society that beckons and taunts from the great and spacious building. Many years ago when Shauna and I were living in another part of the country, a good friend who was then serving as a bishop shared with me an experience he had just had. He indicated that he had been working for a few years with a man in his ward who was a solid citizen, a valued neighbor, a Christian gentleman, but a man who had wrestled with the use of tobacco all his mature life. He was married to an LDS woman of great faith, whose life was exemplary and who yearned for the day when her husband could put away his addiction, attend the temple, and be sealed to her.

My friend the bishop explained that one day he had a visit from this particular brother. In the meeting, the man said, "Bishop, I just spent many hours listening to a series of gospel lectures. I came away inspired, edified, fired up to live the gospel and be a new person. And after a great deal of thought, I have concluded that if I could only make my calling and election sure, I would have the strength to stop smoking."

The bishop was stunned and for a moment was at a loss for words. He finally managed to reply that perhaps, just perhaps, the man might have allowed the cart to move ahead of the horse. They then had a lengthy discussion of which things come first. Another way to put this is to suggest that the blessing of having one's calling and election made sure does not come through flash-in-the-pan, spiritual marathon sessions or higher gospel crusades, nor will we receive the assurance of eternal life through becoming obsessed with making our calling and election sure. If our minds are riveted on fundamentals, our hearts set upon the foundational principles and practices of pure religion (see James 1:27), our mind and heart focused on seeing and feeling about things as the Lord and his anointed servants do, and our temple recommends current and used regularly, then we are on course to gain eternal life.

We know from the marvelous revelation given to the Prophet Joseph Smith as he wrote to the Saints from Liberty Jail that if we can but learn to operate with the priesthood humbly and charitably, using persuasion, long-suffering, gentleness, meekness, unfeigned love, kindness, inspired reproof, and virtuous thoughts, "then shall thy confidence wax strong in the presence of God; and *the doctrine of the priesthood shall distil upon thy soul as the dews from heaven*. The Holy Ghost shall be thy constant companion, and thy scepter an unchanging scepter of righteousness and truth; and thy dominion shall be an everlasting dominion, and without compulsory means it shall flow unto thee forever and ever" (D&C 121:41–46; emphasis added).

These are deep and profound truths, almost too deep, too profound, to give voice to them, to explain them. Some things we can only feel as the Spirit prompts us or enlightens our minds. God and the things of God—including and especially what the scriptures refer to as the "doctrine of the priesthood" (D&C 121:45)—are either revealed or they remain forever unknown (see 1 Corinthians 2:11–14; McConkie, *Ensign*, May 1982, 32–34).

Our Lord and Savior grew up with his brethren, served under his stepfather, Joseph (JST Matthew 3:24–26), and was taught myriads of things by his mother, Mary, and other wise men and women in Nazareth. There were, however, some matters that no mortal person could teach the young Jesus, sacred matters that only God his Father and the Holy Spirit could teach him (see JST Matthew 3:25). Likewise, there are principles and beliefs and insights that come only by divine revelation (1 John 2:27; Moroni 10:5).

As our lives begin to be conformed to the principles of righteousness and proper priesthood governance, and as we make the significant decision that it is the kingdom of God or nothing, that we will serve God at all hazards, then our Heavenly Father will make known to us sacred, saving, and soul-satisfying truths: that our lives are in order; that the course in life we are pursuing is according to his will; that he is pleased with our earthly offering; and, eventually, that our salvation is secure. We will have achieved true greatness. And what is that? President Joseph F. Smith taught: "To do well those things which God ordained to be the common lot of all mankind, is the truest greatness" (*Gospel Doctrine*, 285).

Another way of describing what lies ahead for the faithful is to say that we are foreordained not only to attend to our own sanctification and that of our loved ones but also to contribute to the preparation of this earth to receive its rightful Ruler. And so, what is our task now, today? It is to put our homes in order—to put away anger and hostility, to jettison unkindness and belittling comments, to avoid all forms of pouting and littleness of soul. In short, we must learn to love our wives and children more than we love ourselves. It is to look for and search out ways that we can be more diligent as priesthood holders—as men of God worthy to bless the sick and administer comfort to the bereaved and broken in spirit, as models and examples to boys and new converts, as caring and devoted home teachers, as members of the community who are bold enough to let their voice be heard in a world that is sliding toward Sodom.

The apostle Paul put things into proper perspective for Christian disciples in 1 Corinthians 13 when he taught that charity, or the pure love of Christ, is the highest and greatest and grandest spiritual acquisition, the "more excellent way" (1 Corinthians 12:31), that which true followers of the Lord Jesus Christ seek and strive for all their days. He taught powerfully that men and women might speak in tongues, prophesy, possess all knowledge, regularly care for the poor, and even die willingly for the faith—and still not be possessed of charity. Why? Because we can give without truly loving in God's way, but we cannot love without giving. Charity is a gift or fruit of the Spirit that must be bestowed, given to us, by God. Charity is a sanctifying influence in our lives, a sacred endowment that gradually transforms us into the sons and daughters of God. Charity is that which prepares us for the day when we will see God as he is, since we will have become like him (see Moroni 7:48). This love is vital not only for the work we are called to do as priesthood holders in mortality but will be evident in the lives of those who go on to glory after this life.

Respected New Testament scholar N. T. Wright has written: "The point of 1 Corinthians 13 is that love is not our duty; it is our destiny. It is the language Jesus spoke, and we are called to speak it so that we can converse with him. It is the food they eat in God's new world, and we must acquire the taste for it here and now. It is the music God has written for all his creatures to sing, and we are called to learn it and practice it now so as to be ready when the conductor brings down his baton. It is the resurrection life, and the resurrected Jesus calls us to begin living it with him and for him right now" (*Surprised by Hope*, 288).

And so for now we strive to purify our lives and work toward that day when it can truly be said of us that we are "a royal priesthood, an holy nation, a peculiar people" (1 Peter 2:9). The following words from President Gordon B. Hinckley inspire me to be the man my wife and children and grandchildren deserve: "How magnificent a figure, how royal a character is a man who has been ordained to that priesthood which is called Melchizedek after the great high priest of Salem, who walks with dignity and yet with humility before his God, who lives with respect and appreciation for his associates, who turns his back upon the temptations of the adversary, who becomes a true patriarch in his home, a man of kindness and love, who recognizes his wife as his companion and a daughter of God, and his children as those for whom he has a God-given responsibility to nurture and lead in righteousness and truth. Such a man need never hang his head in shame. He lives without regret. Men may speak of him as they will, but he knows that God knows his heart and that it is pure and unsullied" (*Teachings of Gordon B. Hinckley,* 486).

We become sanctified as we learn to yield our hearts to God (see Helaman 3:35). President Brigham Young's plea for us was simple: "Let us submit to him, that we may share in this invisible, almighty, God-like power, which is the everlasting Priesthood" (*Journal of Discourses,* 3:259). Joshua's words to ancient Israel seem just as appropriate to modern Israel, especially those called to speak and act in the name of Jehovah: "Sanctify yourselves: for tomorrow the Lord will do wonders among you" (Joshua 3:5).

May we serve willingly and nobly, purely and happily, and then may we stand still and see the salvation of the Lord.

REFERENCES

Andersen, Neil L. "Spiritual Whirlwinds." *Ensign,* May 2014, 18–21.

Backman, Milton V., Jr. *American Religions and the Rise of Mormonism.* Salt Lake City: Deseret Book, 1965.

———. *The Heavens Resound: A History of the Church in Ohio, 1830–1838.* Salt Lake City: Deseret Book, 1983.

Ballard, Melvin J. *Melvin J. Ballard, Crusader for Righteousness.* Salt Lake City: Bookcraft, 1966.

Benson, Ezra Taft. *Teachings of Ezra Taft Benson.* Salt Lake City: Bookcraft, 1988.

Carter, Stephen L. *The Culture of Disbelief: How American Law and Politics Trivialize Religious Devotion.* New York: HarperCollins, 1993.

Chesterton, G. K. *St. Thomas Aquinas.* New York: Sheed & Ward, 1954.

Christofferson, D. Todd. "The Doctrine of Christ." *Ensign,* May 2012, 86–90.

———. "Justification and Sanctification." *Ensign,* June 2001, 20–22.

Covey, Stephen R. *Spiritual Roots of Human Relations.* Salt Lake City: Deseret Book, 1970.

Eusebius. *The History of the Church.* Translated by G. A. Williamson.

Introduction by Andrew Louth. Rev. ed. New York: Penguin Books, 1965.

Eyring, Henry B. "A Priceless Heritage of Hope." *Ensign,* May 2014, 22–25.

Hales, Robert D. "'If Ye Love Me, Keep My Commandments.'" *Ensign,* May 2014, 35–38.

Hedges, Andrew H., Alex D. Smith, and Richard Lloyd Anderson, eds. *Journals, Volume 2: December 1841–April 1843.* Vol. 2 of the Journals series of The Joseph Smith Papers, edited by Dean C. Jessee, Ronald K. Esplin, and Richard Lyman Bushman. Salt Lake City: Church Historian's Press, 2011.

Hinckley, Gordon B. "Believe His Prophets." *Ensign,* May 1992, 50–53.

———. "The Continuous Pursuit of Truth." *Ensign,* April 1986, 2–6.

———. "Don't Drop the Ball." *Ensign,* November 1994, 46–49.

———. *Teachings of Gordon B. Hinckley.* Salt Lake City: Deseret Book, 1997.

———. "The Work Goes On." *Ensign,* May 2001, 4–6.

Holland, Jeffrey R. "'Lord, I Believe.'" *Ensign,* May 2013, 93–95.

———. "Our Most Distinguishing Feature." *Ensign,* May 2005, 43–45.

———. "Prophets, Seers, and Revelators." *Ensign,* November 2004, 6–9.

Hunter, Howard W. "Being a Righteous Husband and Father." *Ensign,* November 1994, 49–51.

———. "The Great Symbol of Our Membership." *Ensign,* October 1994, 2–5.

Hymns of The Church of Jesus Christ of Latter-day Saints. Salt Lake City: The Church of Jesus Christ of Latter-day Saints, 1985.

Journal of Discourses. 26 vols. Liverpool: F. D. Richards & Sons, 1851–86.

Journal History of The Church of Jesus Christ of Latter-day Saints. Salt Lake City, Utah, 23 February 1847.

Kimball, Spencer W. "Privileges and Responsibilities of Sisters." *Ensign,* November 1978, 102–6.

——. *Teachings of Spencer W. Kimball.* Edited by Edward L. Kimball. Salt Lake City: Bookcraft, 1982.

Lectures on Faith. Salt Lake City: Deseret Book, 1985.

Lee, Harold B. *Stand Ye in Holy Places.* Salt Lake City: Deseret Book, 1974.

——. *Teachings of Harold B. Lee.* Edited by Clyde J. Williams. Salt Lake City: Bookcraft, 1996.

——. "Understanding Who We Are Brings Self-Respect." *Ensign,* January 1974, 2–6.

——. *Ye Are the Light of the World.* Salt Lake City: Deseret Book, 1974.

Lewis, C. S. *Mere Christianity.* New York: Touchstone, 1996.

Maxwell, Neal A. *A More Excellent Way.* Salt Lake City: Deseret Book, 1967.

——. "Out of Obscurity." *Ensign,* November 1984, 8–11.

McConkie, Bruce R. "The Doctrine of the Priesthood." *Ensign,* May 1982, 32–34.

——. "God Foreordains His Prophets and His People." *Ensign,* May 1974, 71–73.

——. *A New Witness for the Articles of Faith.* Salt Lake City: Deseret Book, 1985.

——. "Succession in the Presidency." Brigham Young University devotional, January 8, 1974. Available at speeches.byu.edu.

McConkie, Joseph Fielding. "The Gathering of Israel and the Return of Christ." *Sixth Annual Church Educational System Religious Educators' Symposium,* 3, 5.Brigham Young University, August 1982. Salt Lake City: The Church of Jesus Christ of Latter-day Saints, 1983.

McConkie, Joseph Fielding, and Robert L. Millet. *Doctrinal Commentary on the Book of Mormon.* 3 vols. Salt Lake City: Bookcraft, 1987–92.

McKay, David O. Conference Report, April 1907, 10–14.

——. Conference Report, October 1912, 119–23.

——. Conference Report, April 1962, 5–9.

——. Conference Report, October 1965, 103–6.

Monson, Thomas S. "The Call of Duty." *Ensign,* May 1986, 37–39.

Morrison, Alexander B. *Turning from Truth: A New Look at the Great Apostasy.* Salt Lake City: Deseret Book, 2005.

Nelson, Russell M. *Perfection Pending.* Salt Lake City: Deseret Book, 1998.

Nibley, Hugh. *Since Cumorah.* Salt Lake City: Deseret Book, 1970.

Oaks, Dallin H. "Family History: In Wisdom and in Order." *Ensign,* June 1989, 6–8.

——. "The Keys and Authority of the Priesthood." *Ensign,* May 2014, 49–52.

——. "No Other Gods." *Ensign,* November 2013, 72–75.

Packer, Boyd K. "Covenants." *Ensign,* May 1987, 23–25.

——. "The Least of These." *Ensign,* November 2004, 86–88.

——. *That All May Be Edified.* Salt Lake City: Bookcraft, 1982.

——. "These Things I Know." *Ensign,* May 2013, 6–8.

——. *The Things of the Soul.* Salt Lake City: Bookcraft, 1996.

——. "What Every Elder Should Know—and Every Sister As Well: A Primer on Principles of Priesthood Government." *Ensign,* February 1993, 6–13.

Palmer, Lee A. *Aaronic Priesthood through the Centuries.* Salt Lake City: The Church of Jesus Christ of Latter-day Saints, 1964.

Penrose, Charles W. Conference Report, April 1921, 9–17.

Phillips, J. B. *The Young Church in Action.* London: Collins, 1955. Cited in Morrison, *Turning from Truth,* 51–52.

Pratt, Orson. *The Holy Spirit.* In *A Series of Pamphlets.* Liverpool: Franklin D. Richards, 1852.

——. *The True Faith.* In *A Series of Pamphlets.* Liverpool: Franklin D. Richards, 1852.

Pratt, Parley P. *Key to the Science of Theology.* Salt Lake City: Deseret Book, 1978.

Richards, LeGrand. *A Marvelous Work and a Wonder.* Salt Lake City: Deseret Book, 1950.

Roberts, B. H. *The Gospel and Man's Relationship to Deity.* Salt Lake City: Deseret Book, 1966.

Romney, Marion G. *Look to God and Live.* Salt Lake City: Deseret Book, 1971.

Smith, Hyrum M., and Janne M. Sjodahl. *Doctrine and Covenants Commentary.* Salt Lake City: Deseret Book, 1965.

Smith, Joseph. *History of The Church of Jesus Christ of Latter-day Saints.* Edited by B. H. Roberts. 2d ed. rev. 7 vols. Salt Lake City: The Church of Jesus Christ of Latter-day Saints, 1932–51.

——. *Joseph Smith.* Teachings of Presidents of the Church series. Salt Lake City: The Church of Jesus Christ of Latter-day Saints, 2007.

——. *The Words of Joseph Smith: The Contemporary Accounts of the Nauvoo Discourses of the Prophet Joseph.* Edited by Andrew F. Ehat and Lyndon W. Cook. Provo: BYU Religious Studies Center, 1980.

Smith, Joseph F. *Gospel Doctrine.* Salt Lake City: Deseret Book, 1971.

——. "In the Presence of the Divine." *Messages of the First Presidency of The Church of Jesus Christ of Latter-day Saints.* Edited by James R. Clark. 6 vols. Salt Lake City: Bookcraft, 1965–75.

Smith, Joseph Fielding. Conference Report, April 1970, 58–60.

——. Conference Report, October 1970, 91–92.

——. *Doctrines of Salvation.* 3 vols. Compiled by Bruce R. McConkie. Salt Lake City: Bookcraft, 1954–56.

Snow, Lorenzo. *The Teachings of Lorenzo Snow.* Edited by Clyde J. Williams. Salt Lake City: Bookcraft, 2012.

——. "Address to the Saints in Great Britain." *Millennial Star* 13, no. 23 (1 December 1851): 362.

Sperry, Sidney B. *Paul's Life and Letters.* Salt Lake City: Bookcraft, 1955.

Taylor, John. *The Gospel Kingdom.* Selected by G. Homer Durham. Salt Lake City: Bookcraft, 1964.

——. *The Mediation and Atonement of Our Lord and Savior Jesus Christ.* Salt Lake City: Deseret News, 1882.

——. *John Taylor.* Teachings of Presidents of the Church series. Salt Lake City: The Church of Jesus Christ of Latter-day Saints, 2001.

Top, Brent L. *The Life Before.* Salt Lake City: Bookcraft, 1988.

Uchtdorf, Dieter F. "Come, Join with Us." *Ensign,* November 2013, 21–24.

——. "Grateful in Any Circumstances." *Ensign,* May 2014, 70–77.

——. "'Lord, Is It I?'" *Ensign,* November 2014, 56–59.

Widtsoe, John A. "The Worth of Souls." *Utah Genealogical and Historical Magazine,* October 1934, 190.

Wright, N. T. *After You Believe: Why Christian Character Matters.* New York: Harper One, 2010.

——. *Surprised by Hope: Rethinking Heaven, the Resurrection, and the Mission of the Church.* New York: Harper One, 2008.

INDEX

ABOUT THE AUTHOR

Robert L. Millet, Coordinator of Religious Outreach and former dean of Religious Education at Brigham Young University, is a professor emeritus of ancient scripture. After receiving bachelor's and master's degrees from BYU in psychology, he earned a PhD from Florida State University in religious studies. He has served in The Church of Jesus Christ of Latter-day Saints as a bishop, stake president, and member of the Materials Evaluation Committee. Brother Millet is a beloved speaker and the author of numerous books. He and his wife, Shauna, are the parents of six children.